How to Reach Millions with Artful PR

How to Reach Millions with Artful PR

What They Don't Teach You in Marketing School

Dana Dobson

ISBN 13: 9781537788739
ISBN 10: 1537788736
Library of Congress Control Number: 2017902054
CreateSpace Independent Publishing Platform
North Charleston, South Carolina

Printed in the United States of America

"To be far from the madding crowd is to be mad indeed."

—*A.E.* Coppard

Table of Contents

Introduction

Public relations, practiced properly, is an art. And, like art, everyone may not have the talent for it, or an understanding of it, or even a liking of it, but everyone who's in business needs it. With this book, I hope to ignite your passion.

Art is a creative endeavor. We learn the fundamentals from skilled instructors, then take those teachings and mold them until they become our own, unique expression of our "professional being" in the world.

At any given time, there are millions of people who resonate with you and want what you offer. What keeps them at a distance is that they don't know you exist—yet. The trick is to get word to them somehow, effectively, efficiently and exponentially, without spending every last dime in your pocket. That's what publicity, a jewel in the PR crown, is for. Be assured: The audience you need is out there, affordably. Your public awaits.

This book is written by someone who believes that PR might be one of the best things you can do for your business if you want to achieve sustainable success. Whether you use PR on its own as your key outreach strategy, or whether your PR works in concert with the numerous other marketing options at your disposal, getting your name out there with help from the media attracts substantial attention from the marketplace that far exceeds that of your less enlightened competitors.

I'm going to teach you how to get publicity and market your content by showing you how to position yourself or your business in the media spotlight and how to leverage the resulting attention to reach the audiences without whom you cannot succeed.

You're going to learn how to engage the media to help you spread your name and message far and wide to the target audiences who don't yet know about you or how fabulous you are. If you already practice PR in your business, this book will hone your skills and reveal opportunities you didn't know existed. If you don't know how or why to use publicity and content strategy, fasten your seatbelts. I will pull back the proverbial curtain so that you can step in and partake in the feast.

It's a universal truth that everything in this world is possible with the help of other people. All of us are connected. People put you in touch with life-changing opportunities, and they also spread the word. Never underestimate the human social network and how its attitudes and behaviors affect the decision-making process. Word-of-mouth is the number one reason why people decide to do business with you.

Remember that shampoo commercial from the 1980s? "I told two friends about Faberge Organics shampoo, and they told two friends, and they told two friends, and so on, and so on…" Word spreads like a virus, its cells multiplying and growing until that fateful, wonderful day when someone you meet at a party says, "Hey! I've heard good things about you! Let's dance!"

At any given time, there are millions of people who resonate with you and want what you offer. What keeps them at a distance is that they don't know you exist—yet.

Media coverage, combined with the implied endorsement of industry recognized thought leaders, provides the best environment for word-of-mouth transmission. Journalists are people who have the skills and audiences to help you achieve your vision for yourself and your business by making you, if not semi-famous, then at least worth getting to know.

People do business with people they know, like and trust. When you're able to successfully earn the respect of information gatekeepers and messengers, you open up the floodgates and warm leads rush in. If this torrent of success is what you want, read on.

There are thousands of books on the market about how to get attention for your business. It makes sense—most public relations people are good writers who are skilled in the art of promotion. What's different about this book is that it's a deeper dive into working with journalists than I've seen in most of the "how to do PR" books out there. Your ability to understand the media mindset and what makes a good story are mission critical. What's wonderful is that it's easier than you think, as long as you work it.

There are many moving parts to a successful PR program. You'll need to create pertinent content that is captivating to the media and their audiences. With time and research, you'll assemble a database of media contacts who need your content. You'll know the kinds of stories they're looking for, and you'll keep your relationship with them alive by being a reliable resource of quality information, even if you don't personally benefit from sharing your expertise.

You'll need to become crystal clear about the value of "personal brand." It takes a close examination of your strengths, passion and knowledge as an individual or as an organization. The more finely honed your brand is, the stronger your opinions and commitment to providing service to the world, and the more confident you are about your unique distinctiveness, the more the media will want to work with you. I can't wait for the day when you step into your brand, watch it soar past the tipping point and go viral. It's a high. (Warning: May become addicting.)

Like anything worth its salt, achieving frequent exposure through the various media outlets takes time and commitment. You can do the work yourself, recruit a member of your team, or hire someone who's been trained as a journalist, knows the intricacies of the media mindset and knows a great opportunity for capturing audience interest when she or he sees one.

However you decide to handle the publicity part of your communications outreach, by reading this book you will become empowered by the knowledge I give you to spot the great opportunities and how to leverage them to achieve the greatest exposure possible. You may not realize it, but you are sitting on a gold mine—a vast, untapped treasure. All that's needed to get to the mother lode is to dig, a few tiny shovels full a day, with patience, persistence and a dab of passion. You'll get where you want to go. I promise.

Win free tuition to the PR Breakthrough™ Publicity Boot Camp

There's a quiz at the end of each chapter. Get a 100 percent score on each and every quiz for a chance to win free tuition to a future PR Breakthrough™ Publicity Boot Camp. See a description of the boot camp at the end of the book.

Chapter 1

What is Public Relations?

"You can make more friends in two months by becoming interested in other people than you can in two years by trying to get other people interested in you."

— DALE CARNEGIE

At a recent speaking gig, I asked for a show of hands of who in the audience used public relations in their business. Out of a crowd of around 100 people, about 20 hands went up, and so did my eyebrows. In actuality, the room should have been a sea of waving arms.

Every business uses public relations to some extent, whether they realize it or not. When I asked people why they didn't raise their hands, they gave me reasons that begged for the writing of this book. It's important that you develop a fundamental understanding of what public relations is, and what it is not, before you wade into the waters of publicity and content strategy. Why? First, because without public relations, your business has no soul, and second, you fail to play the biggest card in your deck of professional possibilities.

Public relations is about the way your publics relate to you, and the way you relate to your publics. It concerns itself with the image you project, your sterling reputation, and your leadership brand.

Public relations has existed since ancient times, when humans first began communicating with one another. One's survival depended upon how well he or she was perceived by the members of the tribe. And the tribe itself survived by how well it was perceived by other collectives of humans, whether in mutual cooperation or deadly conflict. "Word" got out that you produced the best clay pots, the most beautiful seashell necklaces, the fastest horses, or the fiercest warriors. Your very survival, i.e., how well you fared in trade and fed your people, depended upon how well you communicated your message to others and the word-of-mouth that followed.

I met a woman the other day who runs a small bookkeeping firm. We were in a group coaching session. When I talked with the group about public relations and content marketing as tactics to stimulate inquiries from prospects, build brand and generate awareness, she shuddered visibly. "What will I do," she asked, "when my phone's ringing all the time? How will I handle the volume?"

As it turns out, she's afraid of drawing attention to herself. Like so many others out there who want to be in business for themselves, she confuses public relations with publicity, and publicity with shameless self-promotion. To her, getting publicity means immodestly shining the spotlight on herself. This is a common misconception that's deeply grounded in the belief that it's morally wrong to stand proud and that publicity is "tooting one's own horn," which is a bad, bad thing in a culture that values the pretense of modesty. News flash: Publicity is not focused on the tooting of horns. It's about getting you the kind of exposure that creates opportunities for your business.

Every business uses public relations to some extent, whether they realize it or not.

It's fair to assume that the last thing you want is to be invisible to potential customers. If you're reading this book, it's because you want people to know you exist, and how to convince them what actions you need them to take so that you can achieve that thing that feeds and rewards your existence, whether you're selling something, sharing ideas, changing behaviors or inspiring them to take up your cause. This is the essence of public relations, stripped to the skivvies. No business or concern can exist without public relations.

Public relations has always been about the transmission of messaging through content development and dissemination, and getting excellent content out to the appropriate individuals or groups in order to achieve mission critical results. Public relations is also concerned with listening to the needs of your various constituencies and creating meaningful dialogue so that relationships are mutually beneficial.

While the methods of communication have changed since ancient times, the root being of public relations has not. The difference is we now have communications technologies and channels that have created staggering levels of opportunity for anyone who wants to get the word out on a massive scale. We can harness and spread content in ways that, even a few decades ago, were unimagined.

Depending on whom you ask, the term "public relations" was coined and designated a profession circa 1900. If you want to know more about the history of public relations, there is a plethora of reading material about it. Let's assume however, that you're not here for a history lesson. Our PR forefathers and mothers have gone to a great deal of effort to develop definitions, establish codes of conduct and create various *modus operandi* so that human resources people can write accurate job descriptions and so that public relations practitioners can articulate exactly what it is they do all day.

Public relations can be defined in numerous ways. Years ago, when I earned my accreditation in public relations (APR) from the Public Relations Society of America, we were required to recite it this way:

> *Public relations is the management function which establishes and maintains mutually beneficial relationships between an organization and the various publics upon which its success or failure depends.* ("Effective Public Relations," Cutlip, Center and Broom.)

I like this definition. It's simpler:

> *Public relations is about creating, curating, managing, distributing and marketing content to support and promote initiatives, recruit media attention and develop brand loyalists.*[1]

I also like this one, even though it's a bit longer:

> *Public relations describes the various methods a company uses to disseminate messages about its products, services, or overall image to its customers, employees, stockholders, suppliers, or other interested members of the community. The point of public relations is to make the public think favorably about the company and its offerings. Commonly used tools of public relations include news releases, press conferences, speaking engagements, and community service programs.*[2]

When we use the term "public relations," it is to describe a communications outreach that is *intentional.* It has a strategy with a desired result. Public relations is a top line management function and discipline. It is not something any business or initiative can do without—it is not an optional activity. Even if you don't draw a box for it on your organizational chart, relations with your publics still exists. It lives in the DNA of your business. It is the articulation and dissemination of your corporate soul.

Your public relations program defines how you wish to be perceived by your key constituencies. It's behind the formulation, articulation and

---

1 http://smallbiztrends.com/2014/08/tweeting-public-relations.html

2 http://www.inc.com/encyclopedia/public-relations.html

conveyance of your "brand." And this brand, in turn, must be infused into the organizational body down to the cellular level. It is manifested in every action, every word, and through every employee.

Public relations has always been about the transmission of messages through content development and dissemination, and getting excellent content out to the appropriate individuals or groups in order to achieve mission critical results.

Thus, when I speak to an audience comprising people who are in business, every hand in the audience should go up when asked, "Do you use public relations?" A better question, might be, "How do you use public relations in your business?" This question, too, provokes a series of answers that reveal a misunderstanding of what public relations actually is.

The Difference Between Advertising, Marketing and Public Relations

Business owners comfortably use the terms "advertising" and "marketing" to describe how they attract people's attention in order to achieve business objectives, but here, too, most people (including people who claim to be marketing experts) lack a refined understanding of these disciplines and how they differ in purpose and scope.

The terms advertising, marketing and public relations are often used interchangeably, although they shouldn't be, and all of them, incorrectly, are used to mean "promotion," as if they were synonymous. All three of these functions have unique distinctions, but increasingly, these lines are blurring and advertising, public relations and marketing are being dumped into the "promotion" bucket. In the case of public relations, this lack of proper distinction is problematic, because the oversimplification blocks out a wide range of other, more ingenious (and less expensive) strategies for building brand.

Here's a look at advertising, marketing and public relations as separate entities. Keep in mind, as we go through this, that all of these things should be evaluated for strategic value and then folded into the fabric of your business. All of them have specific and important uses and strengths, depending upon your business objectives.

Marketing is the soup-to-nuts, high-level function that describes how you will bring a product or service to market. We typically describe marketing with the four Ps: Packaging, pricing, (paid) promotion and place (distribution). What will the product or service look like? What color is it? What will we call it? Who will buy it? Why should they buy it? How much will it cost? Is it cheap, or expensive? Who's going to sell it, and how? How much money will we budget to buy advertising and pay other promotional costs? Who's going to manufacture it? How will we get it into stores?

Marketing needs to be a well-oiled machine, and it has dozens of moving parts, but people compartmentalize it into a single function: promotion. "Promotion" is only one, tiny sliver of marketing to achieve an overarching result: sales.

Under each of the four Ps are a thousand ideas, tasks, considerations, reams of research data, hours of implementation and a small handful of strategic decisions. It includes advertising (commercials, direct mail, billboards, print ads, sponsorships, etc.), market research, graphic design, business development, promotional collateral development, etc.

For the record, some companies, usually the large, old school ones, believe that ***marketing*** and ***sales*** should be separated into different departments. I strongly disagree. Separating them creates siloes that result in morale-busting internal feuds that lead to blaming and finger pointing.

Advertising is a promotional *tactic*. It is but one of the dozens of tools available to you to sell your products or services. The decision of whether to use advertising to promote your product or service is made when the marketing plan is created and how much of a budget you have.

Advertising costs money because you're buying space, audience size, keywords and production. The price depends upon how much exposure you will get and how often you will run the ad. Super Bowl commercials cost millions, not just because of the size of the audience you'll reach, but also because of what it costs to produce the commercial, which is hundreds of thousands of dollars. For the price of a full-page ad in the *Wall Street Journal*, you could purchase a brand new, fully appointed mid-sized automobile. And, of course, running an ad only once is like squeezing a drop of water onto a hot skillet. Poof!

An advantage of advertising is that you can guarantee your ad will appear in the place and at the time you paid for. You also control the messaging in the ad; no outside force or subjective opinion can change any of the copy or graphic design.

A disadvantage of advertising is that people have increasingly become immune to it. On television, commercials can be muted or fast-forwarded through. Traditional newspapers are going out of business because the advertising dollars have moved online. And, we are all exposed to so much advertising in our daily lives that we've begun to tune it out. Increasingly, as more and more channels of information become available, people have become weary of "being sold to."

I'll explain in a later chapter how humans absorb information and make purchasing decisions, but if you plan to have any success with your advertising, you must have a budget that's large enough to be able to run ads in as many places as possible for as long as possible. Frequency and repetition are absolutely essential, because most people don't even notice your ad until you've run it many times.

The aim of public relations is to educate and communicate, generate awareness, boost public confidence, manage image and reputation, and to convince people to change attitudes and behavior.

Public relations is also a high-level, soup-to-nuts function that aims to achieve organizational states of being and achieve objectives that are not purely focused on the sales or delivery of your products and services to the marketplace.

The aim of public relations is to educate and communicate, generate awareness, boost public confidence, manage image and reputation, and to convince people to change attitudes and behavior. (An area of public relations, called "publicity," is a wonderful way to attract interest and desire to your products and services, and we'll talk about this in the next chapter, but public relations and publicity are not the same thing, the same way as marketing and advertising are not the same thing, or that strategy and tactics are not the same thing.)

Because public relations raises awareness of an organization's existence, and of its products and services, there is a hierarchy of positive effects, one of which is that sales tend to increase. Public relations activities are empirically proven to have a measureable impact on an organization's bottom line.

There are many different areas of focus under the public relations umbrella: media relations, government relations, public policy, investor relations, community relations, shareholder relations, employee relations, internal/external relations, etc.

In any organization, large or small, there are unique sub groups of people, or "publics," with whom a business communicates and forms relationships, and each of them requires a specific strategy and set of messages.

In marketing, the focus is solely to acquire customers, because we want people to buy our stuff. In public relations, our publics are potential customers, existing customers, the media, shareholders, employees, the community, legislators, decision makers, influencers, suppliers—the list goes on. These are our "publics." Building strong relationships, with the ancillary effects of earning trust and credibility is the primary agenda, not "selling," but rather educating, creating value and persuading to believe a certain way.

You'll often hear me say this (and I didn't make it up), that "public relations" should really be called "publics relations," because there's not such thing as a single "public" where business is concerned.

The public relations department does, or ought to do, the lion's share of the content writing, while marketing handles the sales copywriting. Many PR practitioners are former or trained journalists, which gives us an edge in the media relations part of our jobs, but it also means that we're good writers who know how to get to the point and write for our readers. We write newsletters, blogs, white papers, website content, speeches, press kits (explained in detail in a later chapter), press releases, crisis communication plans, annual reports, eBooks, social media profiles, and anything else that's meant to communicate, educate, persuade, build brand or explain.

There are few disadvantages of public relations, because public relations is a necessary business function, as is accounting. It is a box on the org chart that usually reports directly to the CEO. It is a staff function. It interacts with all other departments, or line functions. In contrast, marketing is a "line" function.

Disadvantages of public relations include the lack of control of whether you'll be selected by media outlets as one of the stories they'll cover and how you'll be perceived by target audiences. Another disadvantage mentioned by entrepreneurs and small business owners is the amount of time it takes to execute initiatives and the level of expertise required for seamless execution.

Meanwhile, I invite you to ponder the composition of your "publics" and how you're communicating with them. Every one of them, even if they're not potential "buyers," is important to your survival. Don't forget—include the media as one of your most important target audiences. If you neglect the media, you risk the perils of leaving your very existence to speculation.[3]

---

3 A note about the use of the word, "media" that I thought I should mention if you're a fellow grammar nerd. "Media" is the plural form of the word, "medium." In this book, I use "media" as a singular noun, because when I use it as a plural noun, it sounds awkward to my American ears. If you're British, and say things like, "My family were having an outing," then I apologize and beg your temporary indulgence.

Take the Chapter 1 Quiz

Score 100 percent on every chapter quiz for your chance to win free tuition for the PR Breakthrough™ Publicity Boot Camp:

http://bit.ly/2cJn5Br

Chapter 2

Publicity is Awesomesauce

"Publicity is the life of this culture—in so far as without publicity, capitalism could not survive—and at the same time, publicity is its dream."

— John Berger

The word, "awesomesauce," is in the dictionary. Really! In Internet parlance, it means, "better than awesome." To use it in a sentence: *Publicity is awesomesauce for attracting millions and making your business dreams come true.*

Knowing what it's all about and how to use it will change your life and open up floodgates of potential. Being mentioned or interviewed by the media creates word-of-mouth that helps you achieve goals in ways that far exceed what was possible for you trying to spread your message on your own. To think you've been underutilizing it all this time!

This book aims to make you a publicity expert so that you can reap the as-yet unimagined bounty that enters your life when thousands, even millions, of people discover you, think highly of you and who want to do business with you. Human high regard and a large platform (mailing list, followers, fans, connections, etc.) are keystones in the foundation of your success.

"Publicity" lives under the public relations umbrella. Wikipedia defines publicity as, "gaining public visibility or awareness for a product, service or your company via the [traditional and digital] media." Publicity can make a huge impact on your bottom line. Wielded skillfully and with regularity, publicity builds empires, creates celebrity, attracts followers, sells out inventory, establishes dominance and packs concert halls. On the other hand, "bad" publicity has ruined careers, destroyed reputations and lost elections. Publicity is Thor's hammer, with the power to create, transform—or destroy.

I'll admit I'm a zealot, but only because I have witnessed firsthand what publicity can do. A skilled publicist is an artist who can summon the will of the masses to do her bidding with nothing but a computer, some well-chosen words that are boosted by journalists and viral word of mouth.

Publicity and media relations go hand in hand. Just as sales professionals diligently build referral networks to enhance their business development efforts, publicists develop warm relationships with journalists to carry their messages far and wide. You must learn to love and respect journalists. They are the ones who help you get publicity by sharing your messages on their platforms. Be good to them. They are among your best strategic allies.

The power of building audience via publicity was impressed upon me at an early age. My mother spent her life pursuing an acting career on the stage and screen. Both she and my father were college theater arts majors who were always performing in one way or another, whether as actors in community theater productions, at their day jobs, at the Thanksgiving dinner table, or at social gatherings. They liked to be the center of attention, and happily, they had the physical attractiveness and charisma to pull it off. My father was the lord of the long joke, stretching out each plot point into eternity while his audience giggled in anticipation, and he had a beautiful singing voice. They had loads of friends and scrapbooks filled with newspaper articles about their theater performances. My brother, sister and I basked in the reflected glory.

Just as sales professionals diligently build referral networks to enhance their business development efforts, publicists develop warm relationships with journalists to carry their messages far and wide.

I learned early that having an audience means love and acceptance and all kinds of pleasing fringe benefits, like getting to ride one of the floats in the 4th of July parade, dressed like a princess and waving to adoring crowds with a tiny, cupped hand, or modeling plaid skirts with matching tights on Channel 10's early morning Pixanne Show, while someone off-camera told me to "smile!" in an irritated stage whisper. When I performed in dance, theater or piano recitals, and my parents' smiling, adoring faces were in the audience, life was worth living and all was right with the world. I learned that audience equals positive emotional payoff.

The Beatles phenomenon demonstrated the power of the crowd. The Fab Four's audience comprised teenagers who were driven into a screaming frenzy by flawlessly executed publicity campaigns. Their concerts sold out to stadiums of fans who clamored, cried, broke through police barricades and body blocked the band's limousines. And, these love-crazed maniacs bought records—millions and millions of them. It was unprecedented.

As a child, I didn't know how the audience attraction sausage was made. I didn't yet know that there were persons unknown behind the curtain, working like mad, planning strategies, calling the local papers, making announcements on the radio or handing out flyers. I didn't know what a "person of influence" or "gatekeeper" was. All I knew was that having an admiring audience had benefits that extended far beyond the basic human need for love and acceptance.

If you're a performer of some kind, someone whose professional life is lived upon the stage, then you understand the necessity of "having an audience" all too well. Without spectators, you don't get paid.

Yet, every business has an audience, does it not? In fact, we have several audiences: those who will buy, those who have bought, those who spread the word, strategic allies who work at our side, and those whose approval is necessary to help us achieve our commercial ends (lawmakers, citizens, donors, etc.).

My favorite audience is "those who spread the word." One of the most gratifying phrases for a business owner to hear is, "Hey! I've heard about you!"

The Big Aha! Moment

I was a drama nerd in high school. I'd always been attracted to the theater, whether I was writing plays, producing them and then performing them in the basement with my brother and sister (audience not required), or hanging around my high school theater department. My high school in suburban Philadelphia had the most wonderful theater and music programs. There was the annual musical, of course, choir performances, a summer children's theater program and the annual "variety show." I played a part in all of these, whether painting sets, performing, or sewing costumes.

The auditorium and all of its associated spaces (green room, rehearsal halls, fabrication shops and dressing rooms) were sanctuaries. We kids were a family, and we all had dreams of one day making names for ourselves in the entertainment industry. We had hopes and dreams, productions to stage, and talented teachers to guide our way. What was lacking was a history of sold-out performances.

In the spring of my junior year, we produced our annual variety show, which was about an hour-and-a-half of skits, musical performances and dance routines. That year's theme was "Alpha and Omega," (the beginning and the end). All of the most talented kids were going to be in it, and we were fairly sure we had a hit on our hands. We believed our show was Broadway caliber, and the world needed to know about it. We intended to exceed all ticket sales expectations. We didn't want our typical audience, a one-third-filled house of parents, grandparents and siblings. No! We wanted to fill the auditorium with non relatives who had *bought tickets*! We were passionate, determined and fearless.

What we'd done in the past to promote the variety show was print hundreds of flyers and distribute them through various means: Every student in the school got one. They were tacked up on school bulletin boards. We asked storekeepers on Lancaster and City Line Avenues to display the flyers in their front windows. We pleaded with our parents to help with word-of-mouth. We made daily announcements over the school's P.A. system.

We knew, though, that we needed to do something drastically different this time if we were going to sell out our show. We needed to find a way to get the word out to hundreds and hundreds of people, going way above and beyond our previous methods of stirring up interest and awareness. After all, we had a big hit on our hands, and all that was necessary was to tell the world about it. We'd built it, and now they would come.

Publicity can make a huge impact on your bottom line. Wielded skillfully and with regularity, publicity builds empires.

But, how? The show was going to open in just a couple of weeks, so there wasn't much time. We were still thinking in a limited way, i.e., that passing out flyers was our most promising option for getting the word out. Where on earth could we pass out flyers to massive amounts of people? Why, Center City, Philadelphia! Of course! Center City was the obviously the most populous place, and it was only a 10-minute train ride from home.

The initial plan was to lug a suitcase of flyers to City Hall, smack dab in the middle of everything, and hand them out to thousands of passersby as they emerged from their high-rise offices and flooded the streets during the lunch hour. We thought an hour or two of doing *that* would positively get the word out that "Alpha and Omega" was the big musical hit of the season.

Still, our plan was missing something. Who was going to pay attention to a bunch of hippie-looking post-adolescents handing out flyers? How could we get their attention without getting ourselves arrested? And then, we realized that, "Duh! We're promoting a show! Let's wear costumes!" I don't know why we chose the Flintstone-like animal skins from our cave man sketch, but three of us put them on and boarded the train.

As expected, Center City bustled. Making our way to one of the massive, arched entrances of the beautiful City Hall building, attracting all kinds of stares, we set up our suitcase and passed out flyers.

A woman with a note pad, wearing a khaki, multi-pocketed safari vest, asked us what we were doing, and why. We explained to the woman that we were promoting our high school variety show, "Alpha and Omega," which was destined to be the hit show of the season. She nodded and smiled and introduced herself as a reporter for the *Philadelphia Inquirer*, the city's most highly circulated daily newspaper.

About an hour later, we noticed that there were three men holding large, black film cameras on their shoulders, pointed at us. These, we later learned, were cameramen from the local television stations. We didn't realize it at the time, but our little publicity stunt was being *covered*.

The next day, an article appeared in the *Philadelphia Inquirer,* and segments about us aired on evening news programs. The combined reach for all of this exposure was more than a million readers and viewers. As a result, our little high school variety show sold out. Was it the big hit of the season? For us, it was.

The lesson of this experience for me was that there is a direct correlation between the number of people whose attention you attract and the likelihood that you will achieve your business goals. Our goal was to sell more tickets by getting the word out to greater amounts of people with a publicity stunt. We succeeded.

NOTE: I do not think that the huge exposure enticed those strangers on the street to buy tickets to our high school amateur variety show. Rather, I believe the media attention provoked our fellow students and their families to attend, because it boosted our credibility 10-fold. The coverage awakened interest in an audience often called, "the silent majority" or "lurkers," and compelled them to emerge from the shadow of inactivity.

Publicity is the most effective way of attracting new audiences. It's critical to business success to be recognized, have a strong public identity and a trusted brand. Customers are more likely to buy from you if they remember and think well of you when it's time to make a purchase decision.

Take the Chapter 2 Quiz

Score 100 percent on every chapter quiz for your chance to win free tuition for the PR Breakthrough™ Publicity Boot Camp:

http://bit.ly/2f2VpcO

Chapter 3

The Battle for Your Mind: How Humans Make Decisions

"People are very busy; they are so busy that when they walk in the crowds they see no one, no one but themselves; they hear no voice, no voice but their own voice!"

— *Mehmet Murat Ildan*

"If we think we have reasons for what we believe, that's often a mistake. Our beliefs and our wishes and our hopes are not always anchored in reasons."

— *Daniel Kahneman*

To be a bona fide public relations professional or communications expert, you must have a solid, scientifically grounded understanding of human behavior. Building mutually beneficial relationships with target audiences is a lot more complicated than dreaming up catchy taglines or throwing out messages that *we* think are important for people to hear.

Despite the fact that we all have sophisticated electronic devices in our pockets, we're really just a bunch of primitive, survival focused herd animals. Irrationality is in our DNA. It's science. You shouldn't assume that people make choices or form beliefs logically. There is a continuous war in our minds, where intuition and logic are fighting for control over our decisions and challenging our sanity.

Daniel Kahneman, Ph.D., professor emeritus of psychology and public affairs emeritus at the Woodrow Wilson School and the Eugene Higgins Professor of Psychology Emeritus at Princeton University, has conducted extensive, ground-breaking research on human decision-making in collaboration with the late Amos Tversky, a cognitive and mathematical psychologist. Their work, which won the 2002 Nobel Prize in economic sciences (there is no prize in psychology), proves that our minds don't work the way we think they do.

Kahneman explains that there are two systems of thinking. One is the logical part of your mind, of which you're unaware. It's capable of analyzing problems and coming up with rational answers. But problem solving takes lots of energy, and as the day goes by, the mind gets tired, slows down and becomes lazy.

The other part of the mind, dubbed by Kahneman as "the stranger within," is always in control. It is hidden—we're not aware of it. Too often, it makes most of the decisions before our logical mind even has a clue of what's going on. That's when we run into what psychologists call, "cognitive biases."

That's where the irrational part of our nature kicks in, when cognitive bias appears. Because of our biases, we act impulsively, are easily influenced by what others think, and spend money impulsively on all kinds of crazy things. The stranger within is a silent, whirring machine that's responsible for our beliefs, decisions and opinions. When your logical mind is finally invited to the conversation, it invents reasons why you should think or believe something.

Cognitive bias affects every one of us, whether we are buying a car, curing cancer, building rockets, choosing outfits or traveling in a foreign country. No one is immune. While researching this chapter and reading articles online, I noticed that several of the articles were illustrated with pictures of sheep. It made me smile. We all get that metaphor, don't we, that humans are being likened to submissive herd animals, easily swayed by barking dogs and putty in the hands of manipulative individuals or benevolent shepherds.

Cognitive biases most often affect our thoughts about money. Experts called "behavioral economists" have proven that we don't make financial decisions based on logic. They are studying how to create a system that helps humans make more solid financial decisions.

Dr. Laurie Santos, a Yale University psychologist, studied monkeys to see if monkeys had the same biases as humans, and how deep seated they were. Her experiment, "Monkeynomics," showed that monkeys make the same "loss aversion" mistakes about money that humans do. I'll get to that in a minute.

This demonstrates that much of our behavior has existed since the dawn of time and it seems unlikely that we can ever change it. We can try to understand it, though. Merchants and marketers have used our biases to extract money from us for centuries.

Let's take a look at all the different cognitive biases we humans have. It's a wonder that most of us can walk and chew gum at the same time.

Confirmation bias is the tendency to look for information that confirms what we already know. Think of a conservative, angry, right wing Republican who lives her life receiving and sending out emails that expose all Democrats as criminals and liars. She and the folks within her sphere are extremely selective in what they'll accept as "truth," because what they find and share with one another consistently validates their beliefs. The reverse is true, too.

Hindsight bias is also called the, *"I knew it all along"* bias, or as *"creeping determinism."* It's the inclination, after an event has occurred, to see it as having been predictable, even though there was n reasonable basis for predicting it. How many times have you slapped the palm of your hand against your forehead and said to yourself, "I *knew* that would happen!" How many times have you felt you understood what actually happened "in hindsight?" How often do we ignore our intuition in the moment in favor of making a decision that our conscious, logical mind rationalized?

Baruch Fischoff, Ph.D., a distinguished professor of social and decision sciences at Carnegie Mellon University, conducted an experiment in hindsight bias that explains why people believe what they read, see or hear. He gave participants a short story with four possible outcomes, one of which they were told was true, and then asked the participants to rate the likelihood of each particular outcome. Whichever outcome they were told was true was the one participants chose as being the most likely.

> ***Cognitive bias affects every one of us, whether we are buying a car, curing cancer, building rockets, choosing outfits or traveling in a foreign country.***

Halo effect. This is a cognitive bias in which an observer's overall impression of a person, company, brand or product influences the observer's feelings and thoughts about that entity's character or properties. The opposite is the "horns effect."

For example, a person's attractiveness produces a halo effect. Scientists have proven in the lab that an attractive person is likely to be perceived as nice, or better than you, or intelligent, trustworthy and friendly. We think that people who are attractive lead happier lives, have happy marriages, are better parents and are more successful professionally. Attractive candidates are more likely to win elections or get promoted at work.

Conversely, the ***reverse halo effect*** is when people allow an undesirable trait to influence their evaluation of other traits. For example, attractive defendants in court are likely to be punished more severely than unattractive ones. It also affects some teachers' treatment of students and how they're evaluated.

If your brand is trustworthy and strong, and you have a loyal following, the halo effect can protect your reputation in the event of a crisis.

The ***spotlight effect*** is when people believe they are noticed more than they actually are. We are the center of our own worlds, and we forget that we're not at the center of everyone else's. This is very common. We can't help it. Here are some prime examples:

* You're going through a difficult patch in your life, and you assume you're being singled out by the universe for special punishment.
* You overestimate how many other people share your opinions, attitudes and behaviors.
* You're waiting for the bus. The minute you light your cigarette, it appears. You tell yourself you have magical power over the transit system.
* You think people can tell what you're thinking or feeling; conversely, you think you know what another person is thinking or feeling.
* When you're embarrassed, you think the whole world has noticed and is judging you, or worse, laughing behind your back.
* You're in class and very nervous because you didn't read the assignment and you know for sure the teacher is going to call on you.

Next is ***loss aversion***. We're all hard-wired for this one. It's the big concept in economics and decision theory. It says that people's feelings are stronger about the possibility of incurring a loss than what they feel about acquiring gains. They'd rather avoid financial loss than experience financial gain.

Loss aversion explains one of the biggest challenges faced by bank marketers—getting people to switch from their current bank to *your* bank. Even if their bank was mistreating them, charging higher fees and providing fewer options, people wouldn't switch, because "the devil you know is better than the devil you don't."

Marketers attempt to counter loss aversion by offering trial periods, rebates and 30-day money-back guarantees. It creates the illusion of a risk-free purchase. As humans, we don't like to lose, and we fear making wrong decisions. We tend to stick to the status quo, even if we know it's costing us money. We need reassurance, which is why advertising uses language that implies your audience already owns the product and is living the dream. In commercials, we see attractive people actually using the product.

Negativity bias is the notion that, even with equal intensity, things of a more negative nature (such as unpleasant thoughts, emotions or social interactions and harmful/traumatic events) have a greater effect on one's psychological state and processes than do neutral or positive occurrences.

That's why our Facebook timeliness and the 6:00 p.m. newscast is chock full of bad news. We're addicted to it, and the media outlets are simply giving their public what it wants. If you don't want these channels to lower your spirits or dampen your attempts to remain positive, tune it out. The bottom line is, people tend to respond more to negativity than to positivity. Ratings are lackluster when an outlet focuses only on "good news" stories.

The negativity bias also affects social relationships, in that negative information about a person weighs more heavily than the positive. Thus, an honest person who occasionally does dishonest things would be considered a dishonest person.

Think of the political ads you see on television right before an election. People who run political campaigns know that it's in human nature to vote against a candidate because of negative information than they would vote for a person because of positive information. (Interestingly, though, as people age, they seem to prefer positive information over the negative.)

Keeping this relevant to the media and what constitutes the fascination of constant tragedy and disaster in the news feed, and also to branding and being well-thought-of by your constituents, psychologists say that negative events are more easily remembered than positive ones. If something bad happens and you get a negative impression of something (let's hope it doesn't involve something your company said or did), it'll take several positive impressions to wipe out that one negative memory. In relationships, if you and your spouse experience a negative incident, it's going to take many positive incidents to get your relationship back on an even keel.

We are the center of our own worlds, and we forget that we're not at the center of everyone else's.

Availability bias is the tendency to rely on easily available memories to make judgments. In the early 1960s, people were so shaken by the Cuban missile crisis that they built bomb shelters in their backyards. For fear of the world descending into lawlessness because of Y2K, people hoarded canned goods and buried money in their backyards. After a major plane crash, people jump to the conclusion that it's more likely for them to die in a plane crash than in a car accident, and of course, the opposite is true.

Cognitive bias is inescapable, because remember, most of it is going on below the level of our awareness. But it's not the only phenomenon that affects behavior and decision-making. Another major factor is emotion. Without emotion, we cannot make decisions.

It is said, "The heart strings are connected to the purse strings." Our intuition is aroused well before our minds consciously understand what's going on.

Decisions involve making choices, and scientists have studied how people make them. It's fascinating. Let me count the ways.

Priming. We make choices based on how something has been presented to us. In 2001, Frédéric Brochet, a Ph.D. candidate at the University of Bordeaux in Talence, France, turned the tables on wine snobs when he gave two red wines to 54 wine science students. Little did the students know that one of the glasses contained a white wine into which Brochet had added red food coloring. After smelling, sipping and savoring, the students identified it as an excellent red wine. In a similar experiment, participants were given two glasses of red wine. One, they were told, was a very fine, expensive wine. The other, supposedly, was a cheap wine.

Could they tell the difference? What the participants didn't know, however, was that both glasses contained the same, cheap variety, yet they still chose one over another. The experiments show that people believe what they are told, and even our senses of taste and smell are affected.

Choice Overload. Americans, in particular, like the idea of having many options from which to choose; however, having too many choices can be overwhelming and, as a result, they're less likely to buy. In an extremely entertaining and enlightening TED talk called, "How to Make Choosing Easier,"[4] Sheena Iyengar offers suggestions (four Cs) for helping people choose:

1. Offer fewer choices (cut);
2. Make things concrete (help people understand the consequences of each choice)
3. Categorize (put similar items together)
4. Condition for complexity (build from simple to complex)

Iyengar says that, "when you give people 10 or more options when they're making a choice, they make poor decisions, whether it be healthcare, investments, other critical areas, yet still, many of us believe we should make all of our own choices, and seek out even more of them."

Groupthink is a psychological phenomenon that occurs within a group of people in which the desire for harmony or conformity in the group results in an irrational or dysfunctional decision-making outcome. It happens most often when there is a strong, persuasive group leader, when the group is tight and cohesive, or when the group experiences intense pressure from outside influences. Groupthink is evident in rioting, mass hysteria, lynch mobs and party politics. There are many case studies chronicling how groupthink within a company's corporate culture has caused the organization's demise.

4 https://www.ted.com/talks/sheena_iyengar_on_the_art_of_choosing?language=en

Public relations professionals also call this the "bandwagon effect," which is when people decide to jump on board with certain beliefs, fads, and trends because "everyone else is doing it."

Understanding, and having compassion for, human behavior is what sets masterful communicators and leaders apart. People always want to know, "What's in it for me?" When reading your press release or story pitch, your media contact will ask, "Why do I care? Why should my readers care?" People believe what they read and see and hear from credible media sources. Thus, when something positive is said about you in a news story, or when you're introduced as an expert, people believe it to be true. And, they'll believe it, too, when something negative is said about you, which is why you must work tirelessly to earn the trust of your target audiences, and make brand and relationship building one of your highest priorities.

Take the Chapter 3 Quiz

Score 100 percent on every chapter quiz for your chance to win free tuition for the PR Breakthrough™ Publicity Boot Camp:

http://bit.ly/2gokjPo ("o" = zero)

Chapter 4

Communication Formulas, Rules and Principles Governing the Formulation of Artful PR Strategy

"All men can see these tactics whereby I conquer, but what none can see is the strategy out of which victory is evolved."

— Sun Tzu

Now that you know more about what drives human behavior, you will be able to shift the quality of your content away from your own self interests and into a stronger focus on what your *audience* needs and wants. Following are a few more underlying tenets behind communications and content strategy. Here I'll explain more of the "what" behind your communications strategy rather than the how-to aspects. After all, this is a book about using publicity and content strategy to achieve your goals.

Maslow's Hierarchy

One of the most well known principles behind content and communications strategy involves a piece of intellectual property that you may have heard of once or twice: Maslow's Hierarchy of Needs.

Maslow's Hierarchy of Needs is my Niagara Falls.[5] It seems no matter what college course one takes about public relations, marketing or consumer behavior, Maslow's Hierarchy of Needs pops into the curriculum.

However, you need to be familiar with it because it provides a wonderful framework for understanding people's most primal, authentic motivations. When we understand what drives people while they're experiencing the variegated, up and down circumstances of their lives, we can become more effective, enlightened communicators.

In a 1943 paper entitled, "A Theory of Human Motivation," and then more thoroughly in his 1954 book, "Motivation and Personality," Abraham Maslow presented a five-stage model that categorizes how humans establish priorities in order to survive and ultimately develop to their full potential. The model is illustrated as a pyramid, with the largest, most essential survival needs at the bottom. After each level of need is satisfied, a person moves up the pyramid, step by step, to the top.

At the base of the pyramid are the physiological needs, which are most essential to keeping our bodies alive: food, water, shelter, and warmth. Once those needs are met, we can move up to the next level, which is safety and security: financial, health and well-being and protection from physical harm. Then comes belongingness and love, then esteem, and finally, self-actualization.[6] What happens after that is anyone's guess.

Maslow said that every person is capable and has the desire to move up the hierarchy toward a level of self-actualization, but that progress is often derailed by failure to meet lower level needs. Life experiences, including divorce and loss of job, may cause an individual to fluctuate between levels of the hierarchy. It's rare, he says, for someone to reach the level of self-actualization.

---

5 "Niagara Falls" sketch: https://youtu.be/MYP1OBZfFK0

6 See Samples & Resources section for an illustration the Maslow's Hierarchy of Needs pyramid. I can't stand to look at it anymore, but you might like it.

When we understand what drives people while they're experiencing the variegated, up and down circumstances of their lives, we can become more effective, enlightened communicators.

Public relations professionals use Maslow's hierarchy to target the right message to the right audience by understanding where they are on the pyramid and what's important to them. A single mother who's worried about feeding her children has quite different needs than a woman who's concerned about breaking through the glass ceiling or fighting the signs of aging. A dating service might use messages that are about the search for love and belonging. An expensive day spa would appeal to esteem needs such as prestige and exclusivity. Burglar alarm companies, naturally, will appeal to the need for family safety. By reading this book, you are in the level of self-actualization, which is about improving yourself in order to reach your full potential. Tomorrow, when you're at work or in a group of your peers, you may find yourself in the lower rung of esteem—seeking approval and respect.

The A.I.D.A. Formula

The A.I.D.A. formula is another item that crops up frequently in the public relations and marketing curriculums. It's a technique for crafting sales copy, but it still applies in PR when your campaign is about influencing audience behavior. These are the four steps to take your audience through if you want them to behave according to plan:

Attention. You have to attract a person's attention quickly and get his brain to stop in its tracks before it wanders off to the next shiny object. We do this in the subject line of an email, in the headline of a press release, in the title of a white paper and in the first one or two sentences of your text. Before you can get his attention, you need to understand him intimately. What kind of nomenclature or style of language does he use? Are you talking to a surfer dude or a C-Suite executive? What are his most pressing problems or pain points? What is his lifestyle? Does he keep up with the Joneses? What are his values? You need to know what species of fish you're trying to catch so that you can use the right bait.

Interest. Okay, you've lured a few into your net. They're listening. Now it's time to tell them why they should be interested, because their "strangers within" are asking, "Does this have anything to do with me?" You have to give them a reason to stick around to listen to the rest of your message. Keep your paragraphs short. Use bullet points to call out the important points. Hurry up! You're losing them. Don't be boring. Here is the place you show them you understand their situation. For example, it's typical for a life or business coach to share his/her own personal story, if it's juicy and dramatic and has a happy ending—*Years ago, I had $5.42 in my pocket (and a bottle of grain alcohol), but today I'm a trouble-free multi-millionaire thanks to the simple, 12-step program I invented.*

Desire. Now they're hooked. They want to know more. It's time to appeal to their personal needs and wants. Make them see the possibilities. Let them walk in the shoes of their desire, but be careful not to confuse interest with desire. They're not the same thing. In this section, your task is to show them how your solution solves their problems. Give them tangibles, testimonials (social proof) and evidence to back up your claims. How, exactly, is your solution going to impact their lives or their bottom lines?

Action. You're a genius. They want it, and they want it now. This is the call to action. Tell them what you want them to do, i.e., click here to register, call our toll-free number, visit our website for more information, donate now. Try to think through any reasons why they wouldn't want to pull the trigger. Remember the "loss aversion" bias? Offer a money-back guarantee. Offer a payment plan. Do your best to remove any barriers that might prevent them from taking action.

The 10 80 10 Rule

This principle states that in any given target audience, 10 percent are raving fans, 80 percent are undecided, and 10 percent aren't at all interested.

10% Raving Fans	80% Undecided — Focus Here —	10% Not Interested

The portion of the audience that is most worth your time and resources are the ones who are undecided. You'll never convince the 10 percent who aren't interested, and the remaining 10 percent love you already.

Attitudes, Opinions and Behaviors

The above three words describe the main goals of communication to our target audiences.

An ***attitude*** is, according to Carl Jung, "a readiness of the psyche to act or react in a certain way." It's how we *feel* about a person, place, thing or event. Attitudes are both conscious and unconscious. People don't always share their attitudes, but when they do, you get insights into how they'll be inclined to receive or react to the information you share, or about your industry or line of expertise. Attitudes can be so deeply ingrained that changing them can be difficult. But, it's not impossible.

An ***opinion*** is that we *think* about something. Opinions are not always formed logically, or by understanding the facts. Many times, opinions are shaped by the wrong or false information. Opinions held individually can be changed with education. Public opinion, on the other hand, is a juggernaut that can harm the success of any business, and it's up to you to understand the power of public opinion and strive to create positive impressions of yourself and your enterprise. The thing with opinions is, they change. They can be formed or withdrawn on a whim. That's why in public opinion polls researchers always allow for a "margin of error," because people will give opinions that don't necessarily reflect what they actually think. More about that later.

Behavior describes the way a person acts or the actions they take. Changing behavior is one of the most frequent aims of public relations, and you've been witness to many of the campaigns aimed at convincing people to take, or stop taking, certain actions. Be alert for these kinds of campaigns so you can recognize and emulate them. Some examples of behavior-changing campaigns include:

* *Wear Your Seatbelts.* There was a time when the wearing of seatbelts in automobiles was not required. When the law changed to make the wearing of seatbelts mandatory, the messaging was everywhere. Many businesses were affected by the new seatbelt laws (it affected their insurance premiums), and they conducted internal campaigns to convince employees to "buckle up" every day.
* *Don't Drink and Drive.* These campaigns continue to be everywhere.
* *Only You Can Prevent Forest Fires.* This campaign, featuring Smokey Bear, was created in 1944. It must be working.
* *Milk is the best way to get calcium into your diet.* Food companies are brilliant at getting people to switch their eating behaviors. We've been seduced into consuming dairy products and thinking glutens are bad. I, myself, am purchasing organic fruits and vegetables as the result of well-crafted public relations campaigns that have effectively shaped public opinion. I have also restricted my consumption of dairy products. This decision is solely based upon the *content* I've read or watched.
* *Don't let the town allow a big-box retailer to build in our community.* There's always some kind of "not in my backyard" (NIMBY) campaign going on. People take action by signing petitions, boycotting retailers or standing in picket lines.

Self Delusion

Why do so many new businesses fail? There are several reasons, of course, but one of the biggest is that they fail to do their research. Don't make this fatal error.

I'll explain various modes of market research in Chapter 17 when I show you how to put together a comprehensive communications plan, but I'm mentioning it now because you should always be putting yourself in the shoes of the people with whom you want to connect: journalists, customers, employees, legislators and/or anyone else who has a vested interest in the success of your endeavors. Without research, you're flying blind, or drinking your own Kool-Aid.

Keeping your mind open to the opinions, attitudes and behaviors of your audience members takes courage. Perhaps an idea you had your heart set on turns out to be something your research reveals isn't ready for market, or that people simply aren't interested. It's a bad idea to launch *anything* until you're fairly convinced by the research that there is a market for it.

No company should be insular, with a wall around it or barricades that separate it from the outside world. While you're producing an output of communication, you must also be receiving input from the outside world on a continual basis. In public relations, we describe the boundaries around us as permeable, and breathing, like the lining of a cell. We inhale feedback from the outside world, and exhale our ideas and output to honor that feedback. We serve our audiences by giving them what they want, or need.

The phrase, "Drinking the Kool-Aid" is often used when a company is so attached to its own products and services that if fails to consider the needs of its customers or journalists. They operate under a shared delusion. I have worked with companies whose belief in their own offerings and philosophies made them blind to the needs of their markets, and worse yet, they offended the various stakeholders upon whom their success and failure depended.

Public opinion, on the other hand, is a juggernaut that can harm the success of any business, and it's up to you to understand the power of public opinion and strive to create positive impressions of yourself and your enterprise.

"Drinking the Kool-Aid" is not the same thing as "team spirit." Passion for one's organizational vision and mission is a wonderful thing—and essential. I'm talking about the C-Suite executive or business owner who forgets their company is there to fulfill an unmet need or provide what their audience actually *wants.*

Consider the Ford Edsel story. The Edsel product launch has gone down in history as a colossal marketing faux pas, or failure to gauge what their customers wanted. There are several reasons for its failure, which I'll explain in greater detail in Chapter 17.

Research the demand for your product or service thoroughly before rolling it out to the market at large. The media had a field day with the Edsel. It became the "fun thing to criticize." If there's any fault whatsoever with your product, how it's delivered, or the quality of your customer service, there could be a storm of outrage in the form of customer complaints in social media or bad reviews from well-intentioned consumer advocacy reporters. Be sure your offering is a well-oiled machine with plenty of support from your friendly, well-trained employees.

Edsel was dubbed, "the wrong car at the wrong time." So, stay away from the Kool-Aid.

The Three Source Rule

Journalists are taught that in order for a news story to be objective and credible, three different sources must be consulted and quoted in a story. Many of the stories they write are about wider issues than just your business alone, and if you've built strong, collaborative relationships with them, you may be one of their regular three sources. Being one of those dependable sources, being "quoted" regularly, is one of your highest goals in establishing relationships with media professionals. In the old days, we used to call this, "being on speed dial," or "in the Rolodex."

The Long Game

There's no such thing as an "instant fix" or "immediate results" in public relations or marketing, unless you're a bank offering a 10 percent interest rate on CDs, which you'd promote via advertising, not publicity. Anything worth having, and keeping, takes time, effort, patience and faith. In order to achieve that wonderful thing called "publicity," you must be willing to do the work smartly and consistently, over time.

There's no "end game." The process never stops. Think of your publicity program as a living, breathing organism that requires daily feeding and regular nurturing. It is something that grows and evolves, suffers pain during the hard times and leaps with joy during abundant times. It's a continuous cycle, but what sustains you is your realization that you must always be communicating with, and pleasing, your audience. All that's needed is a little bit of patience and a lot of determination.

So read on, for now the real lessons begin.

Take the Chapter 4 Quiz

Score 100 percent on every chapter quiz for your chance to win free tuition for the PR Breakthrough™ Publicity Boot Camp:

http://bit.ly/2fPquUR

Chapter 5

The Media Mindset

"I am deeply interested in the progress and elevation of journalism, having spent my life in that profession, regarding it as a noble profession and one of unequaled importance for its influence upon the minds and morals of the people."

— *Joseph Pulitzer*

You don't have to be a journalist to think like one. Journalism is a state of mind, a constant craving to tell stories or to share with others what you've seen firsthand—suffering, injustice, joy, fascinating people—and moreover, tell it in a voice that's uniquely yours. If you keep a diary, or journal, then essentially, you are a journalist.

How I Paid My Dues

My first experience as a journalist was as a general assignment reporter for a small weekly newspaper in Scottsdale, Ariz. It focused on neighborhood issues, schools, local government and community features. In addition to a couple of other reporters, there was a managing editor, an editor, a copy editor, a contingent of print house and delivery people, and a photographer or two. This was in the early 1990s.

In the first few months, my editor dispatched me to cover school board and city council meetings, which most reporters find very boring, but I learned a great deal.

Covering council meetings showed me the power of public opinion and how the bureaucracy works. A couple of them stand out in my memory. One was my first experience with a NIMBY (Not In My Back Yard) campaign, when citizens stormed city council chambers to protest the construction of a Wal-Mart Superstore slated to be built in a posh section of town. City council liked the idea of a big box retailer, because it meant a nice increase in tax revenue.

The citizen opposition was led by an activist soccer mom who argued that increased traffic volume posed a threat to children's safety and the town's peaceful, upscale quality of life. Wal-Mart, they claimed, would bring into their glitzy little burg an "undesirable element," i.e., the stereotypical, oddly dressed "Wal-Mart customer," and in their zip code, where the median price of homes at the time was half a million or more, this was unacceptable. Merchants fretted that Wal-Mart's predatory pricing model would put them out of business, and they had compelling evidence to back up their claims. The citizenry was well organized, and in this case, their ferocity of opposition won the day. During this particular city council meeting, I couldn't write fast enough, and the photographers had a field day.

Journalism is a state of mind, a constant craving to tell stories or to share with others what you've seen firsthand

Another educational city council meeting was when a group of citizens made its case for a new solution to pay for a high-speed light rail transit system. There had been a rallying cry for light rail and increased freeway infrastructure for years in the Phoenix area, but all failed, because no one could, or would, agree on how to pay for it. This group had some compelling, well-researched ideas, and they hoped for the city council's support to take the campaign statewide. They brought in a retinue of experts comprised of attorneys and influential community leaders, and some of the nicest illustrations on foam core display boards I'd ever seen. Despite a stellar presentation compelling enough to change just about anyone's mind, the city council voted against their proposition, and the light rail debate dragged on for years. Afterwards, the city council members scurried away from the press and into the woodwork, leaving no one for me to interview but the pro light rail folks, so they got the last word.

For me, the best stories to write about were the human interest ones, e.g., the man who annually, and gleefully, irritated his neighbors with over the top Christmas light displays; the Italian restaurant franchise that was founded by the children of famed Mama Celeste, whose television commercials famously ended with the tag, "Abbondanza!"; pro golfer Phil Mickelson's ophthalmologist, who was making a name for himself teaching golfers how to up their games by becoming more aware of their peripheral vision. These kinds of stories I liked—triumph of the human spirit, winning through incredible odds, shaking the tree of life—stories that help us see the importance of things, help us be better people, allow us to walk in the shoes of shape shifters and the ones who dare take the bigger leaps.

More important, the *readers* liked the stories. I had a byline, and an audience. When one of my stories appeared about a local business, either their traffic increased or they got phone calls from people they hadn't heard from in years congratulating them on their "success." I learned that businesses could have audiences, too, not just entertainers. Also, I saw that just one little article in the local newspaper created the perception in readers that a business or person was successful.

I next worked as an "experiential journalist" with a sports and fitness magazine. It was my job to involve myself physically in whatever sports- or fitness-related activity to which my editor assigned me. I was sent to scuba-diving classes (loved it), to an orienteering expedition, which is basically you and a compass in the middle of the desert trying to find your way out by following the coordinates of orange flags (loved/hated it), and a few sessions in a local gym training me, a young woman, how to be a boxer (hated it, because I got punched in the head one too many times.) If you ever need desert survival tips, or to learn how to avoid multiple blows to the face, I'm your gal.

I've been a freelance business and feature writer for many years, writing as a frequent contributor on a number of topics: business, parenting, real estate, home building, restaurants, technology, local issues, fitness, food and more. Freelancing gave me flexibility and freedom, but not a lot of money.

That's when the public relations industry reached out to me, and I went to work for PR agencies building audiences and positive reputations for Fortune 500 companies in a wide variety of industries. I learned how to be a publicist, placing my clients' stories with media outlets or attracting media coverage of their events. A high percentage of my story pitches landed, which never seemed like a major feat to me. All I did was put myself in the editor's shoes and ask what I'd do if this story idea came across my desk. Did stories always land? No, but not because the ideas weren't good. There are several other mitigating factors involved in which stories get chosen. I'll explain later.

As a PR professional, I was now on the other side of the barbed wire fence from my journalist friends, who accused me of moving over to the "dark side of the force." PR people get a bad rap, I think, because many people who enter the field aren't trained for the profession. There's a low barrier to entry, so anyone can pop on board and say they "do" public relations. Other than the APR designation confirmed by the Public Relations Society of America, there's no certifying body to enforce a code of ethics or to ensure professional competency. Many have never been journalists or worked in a newsroom, haven't studied human psychology, and can't write well or with the audience in mind. And so, a bunch of bad apples ruin it for the rest of us.

Some people are attracted to the PR profession because, from the outside, PR looks a glamorous job. When I taught "Introduction to Public Relations" at a university, I polled my students to find out why they wanted to go into the field. The majority of them pictured themselves in the sports, entertainment or fashion industries, planning lavish parties and riding in the backs of limousines. Until they took my class, most students never realized that in order to be successful in public relations, one must be a good writer and business strategist. They had the impression that all PR people were fast-talking extroverts, not realizing that many of us are former journalists who prefer to avoid the limelight. Many of us are quiet, deliberate, strategic planners with a nose for news, business acumen, and a passion for reading, research and pitching great story ideas to journalists.

Good content is a journalist's lifeblood.

Good content is a journalist's lifeblood. At any given moment, there's a media outlet searching for a story about your industry, an expert who can answer questions, a heads up about a trend, a new angle on a popular topic, an idea that needs spreading, a new way to use baking soda or coconut oil, an event that's going on in the community, or help explaining a breaking news story.

They *need* you! They *want* to enjoy the benefit of your expertise. You can become skilled at delivering great content to the media and other channels on a frequent and consistent basis.

This chapter is an examination of the people who proudly call themselves, "journalists." Who are they? How did they get that way? Where are they coming from? Should you fear them? Are they out to get you? Are they ignoring you on purpose? How come they don't return your emails or phone calls? Following is a deep dive into the media mindset so that you can get comfortable with how they're trained, what they do, what their skill sets are and how things operate behind the scenes, when they're at work.

Journalism, Then and Now

Newsrooms once employed hundreds of people: photographers, junior reporters, senior reporters, managing editors, copy editors, and wannabe reporters working shifts in the mail room just to get a shot at a profession that held itself to rigorous standards.

Newspapers stayed alive, and profitable, because of advertising. Retailers in particular spent tens of thousands of dollars every week. Marketers depended upon print vehicles as their best way to reach concentrated, local audiences via advertising.

The rise of the Internet has devastated print-based revenue streams. The *Yellow Pages* are a distant memory. B-to-B direct mail has all but been abandoned. Newspaper advertising revenue has decreased, resulting in massive layoffs in all of the traditional media outlets—print, television and radio—because with the rise of the Internet, readers and listeners have more choices than ever to learn about what's going on the world. Many believe magazines will survive the print-based advertising Armageddon, but it's still early. No one knows how all of this will shake out.

Thus, instead of dozens of people in the newsroom to carry out the numerous tasks required to produce a daily newspaper or nightly newscast, there are only four or five. Add to that the burden of the 24/7 news cycle, which means there's a never-ceasing need for quality content and multi-skilled personnel who work around the clock.

Combine that pressure with the fact that, with the rise of the Internet, millions more people have the ability to relay news and story ideas to the media, meaning the strained staff of four or five in the newsroom have email inboxes stuffed to the gills with hundreds of strange, unusable and irrelevant story pitches and press releases. How nice it is when people like you, who understand the media outlets' ravenous need for good content, step up to help.

How Journalists Develop a "Nose for News"

One of the secrets of successful publicity is being able to spot a trend or current event that you can tie into. A story that has great news value is one that will attract the attention and interest of your audience, but more importantly, one that your media contacts will find interesting.

My goal is to get you seeing your business and the marketplace through the eyes of a journalist so that you can recognize a newsworthy idea. Once you have this down, you're going to be able to produce content and build your brand to an effect that's many times greater than anything else you're doing to promote your business.

Not all journalists go to college. A friend of mine had an innate ability to tell a good story on camera. She had a gift for gab, intelligence, and a bright, friendly face. She found work at a local news station right out of high school, and rose through the ranks to become an evening news anchor. Everything else she learned on the job. But that's a rare occurrence. She was a natural, with big talent and a bigger-than-ordinary on-camera persona.

However, most of us learn the craft of journalism in college. During the freshman and sophomore years, we take compulsory classes in sociology, philosophy, psychology, history and political science, because we need to learn how people think and how society operates. We're taught the basics of newswriting—news pyramids, the lead and "nut graphs," how to describe auto accidents and how to speed read the *AP Stylebook* when we need to look up a rule of grammar or whether the word "Internet" ought to be capitalized.

The *AP Stylebook*[7] is the journalist's bible. In journalism school, there were serious repercussions if you didn't adhere to AP style in your story assignments, whether you were being graded by a professor, or later, in the newsroom, when your copy editor chewed you out for not checking your work properly. (Copy editors no longer or rarely exist. Reporters are held highly accountable for any spelling or style errors.)

Keep this in mind when you submit press releases. They must be written in AP style, or else the journalist who's reading it will experience cognitive dissonance and subconsciously (or even consciously) make a judgment about your professionalism or credibility. We can spot an untrained news writer from miles away with the teeniest formatting or

---

7 You can order a copy of the AP Stylebook here: http://astore.amazon.com/prbreakthrough-20

style mistakes. Because of the enormous volume of emails they receive, one typo or poorly formatted press release makes it easy for the journalist to hit the "delete" button. There's just too much junk out there and too little time and patience. Writing your press release like a reporter, using AP style, increases your credibility substantially.

In the junior and senior years of journalism school, we studied political science, statistics, ethics and mass communications law, because we had to understand legal precedents, the specifics of libel and slander, and why it is essential to have and maintain strong ethical standards in a highly corruptible environment.

We learned how to write headlines that summarized a story and fit within the column width. We learned word economy. Some people skim the headlines when they read, and stop there. The better the headline, the more likely it is they'll read the entire story, or at least, the lead paragraph, which contains no more than 45 words and is where all of the important facts are summarized.

We learned the importance of including at least three sources in a story to ensure balanced story telling, and how crucial it is to check our facts. As journalists, they said, our job was to be impartial, and it was our duty to present an objective view of events. In the sacred realm of ethical journalism, which still exists for legitimate journalists, we were trained to believe in, and uphold, the people's right to know the truth. Even if you don't believe that all journalists are unbiased, it doesn't matter. Everything you present to a media outlet must be balanced and backed up by evidence, or the gatekeeper will kick you out.

After graduation, it's dues paying time. We recent grads were given the most grueling assignments, e.g., covering school board and city council meetings. (In episode six of my Media Pro Spotlight podcast, WHYY's Mark Eichmann tells us that in his early years he was assigned to cover school board and city council meetings, and I guffawed with laughter. Now you know why.)

By melding into the world of professional journalism, it was reinforced in us by our learned elders that our jobs were sacred, important, and necessary for a free society, sometimes dangerous, often exciting, and that we, in our own way, were making an important contribution to the world.

Jacks of All Trades

News has always happened around the clock—that's not new. What's new is that people now have access to channels that are broadcasting the latest updates 24/7. We used to have to wait until the 5:30 a.m. TV news program or the delivery of the morning paper. Now we can access the news from any handheld device. Thus, the media never sleeps, and most of the traditional outlets, have built their own online news and social media channels.

Everyone in the newsroom has to wear several hats. Increasingly, there are no "specialists" in a newsroom. Writers now have to be able to take pictures or shoot and edit video, and conversely, photographers must now be able to write, and videographers need to be able to take still shots.

Reporters have to be more careful than ever about checking facts in their stories. Gone are the days when there was an official "fact checker" in the cubicle next door. Because the public has greater access to news and information, they have the greater ability to call journalists on their mistakes with troll-like ferocity.

There's also a new pressure on print journalists to achieve certain levels of online "readership" with their stories. The higher their readership, the better chance of keeping their jobs. To me, this has alarming implications, but that's another story for another time. Suffice it to say that journalists are under high pressure to produce good, quality and relevant content in order to engage and keep audiences.

What is "The Media?"

One way to define media is "communications channels through which news, entertainment, education, data or promotional messages are disseminated."[8]

8 http://www.businessdictionary.com/definition/media.html

There is the "traditional media," which are newspapers, magazines, radio, television, online news sites and the blogosphere, and the "new" media, which is digital. Of course, there are numerous other channels through which we can disseminate content and messaging.

With "traditional media," you are required to curry the favor and interest of journalists before you can gain access and trust. These are the people who are employed by the channel to make decisions on what content is relevant, serves the needs of their audiences, and is in the right place at the right time.

With "traditional media," there are rules of conduct. A level of finesse is required. It's more difficult to get in, and it requires the kind of patience that unnerves the less skilled and those who don't know what they don't know. That's why the vast majority of the market flocked to social media as the promotional channel of choice, which is fantastic for you. Why?

Because it leaves the rest of us, those who have taken the time to learn and apply strong publicity skills, to swim in the open waters and reap ten times the rewards.

Your Business is a Media Outlet

If you're putting out content on a regular basis—videos, blogs, newsletters, etc.—then by definition, you are a media outlet. Presumably, you have a well-defined set of audiences and the resources to perpetually create and distribute information that's valuable, entertaining and educational.

By learning how to work effectively with new traditional media, you can up the ante on your own in-house content generation because you already have a plethora of material in your inventory. What you lack, however, is a bigger audience. When you're distributing your own content, you're dependent upon the limited range of your existing channels, i.e., Facebook fans, LinkedIn connections, Twitter followers and YouTube viewers.

Spend a few extra hours per week cultivating relationships with journalists and tear a giant hole in that thin veil that separates your message with millions of new eyeballs.

Take the Chapter 5 Quiz

Score 100 percent on every chapter quiz for your chance to win free tuition for the PR Breakthrough™ Publicity Boot Camp:

http://bit.ly/2g7R5tl

Chapter 6

Newsworthiness

"Well, news is anything that's interesting that relates to what's happening in the world, what's happening in areas of the culture that would be of interest to your audience."

—Kurt Loder

Finding and telling a good story is everything when it comes to growing your public presence. First, you must be able to recognize what a good story is in the eyes of journalists and the people whose attention you want to get, and whose hearts and minds you want to reach.

According to Dictionary.com, "newsworthy" is an adjective that means, "of sufficient interest to the public or a special audience to warrant press attention or coverage."

On any given day, journalists receive hundreds of requests for coverage for opinions or events that are not newsworthy. Here's a look at what journalists are trained to consider as newsworthy, and what kinds of information the public craves.

The following 12 news determinants will give you guidelines on what makes "news" in which people are interested.

Prominence

A story has prominence when it is attached to a celebrity or person who's in the public eye. If you host an event, and a famous actor, politician or professional athlete is going to be there, the media will be interested, and not just the media, but any of the publics you're trying to attract. Some examples from my experience of how to leverage "prominence" to your advantage are:

* Pay a local sports celebrity to sign autographs at a grand opening.
* Create a community or cause-related event that attracts a celebrity who supports the same or similar cause.
* Collaborate with strategic partners to fund a celebrity appearance at a special event that *you* have created and organized.
* Involve the mayor or other local government officials for groundbreaking ceremonies, official declarations or site tours.

Significance

A story is considered "significant" when large numbers of people—locally, nationally or globally—are affected, such as airplane crashes, natural disasters, multi-vehicle accidents, power outages, terrorist attacks, forest fires or occurrences of national or global importance or popularity. This is also "breaking news."

Stories of significance trump all other news stories. Reports of loss of human life, tragedy or great peril will always take priority over other of the media outlets' commitments to cover your event. For example, if a TV news assignment editor promised to send a unit to your big grand opening, at which Babe Ruth himself was going to appear and autograph baseballs, a nearby catastrophic event would preempt the coverage of your grand opening.

Of course, you have no control over the occurrence of significant events, but it is imperative that you keep current on what's going on in your town, region, country or world so that you can contribute your expertise to the journalists who are covering these stories.

David Meerman Scott coined the term, "newsjacking," which he defines as, "the art and science of injecting your ideas into a breaking news story to get media attention." For example, are you an expert in air traffic control or airplane mechanics who might be able to provide additional insight in the event of a plane crash? Were you on the scene of a major traffic accident or train derailment and willing to share a firsthand personal account? Is your business collecting water and supplies to aid the victims of a devastating natural disaster?

When tragedy strikes, and your products, services or expertise can be of service to humanity, you have an opportunity to earn the trust of, and be of service to, the media and the community at large. Journalists often call upon the experts they trust to help them prepare and tell their stories. You can help by:

* Disagreeing with the report you heard
* Adding a new dimension to it
* Giving examples
* Explaining it
* Predicting the future

Proximity

Local media outlets like to write about or cover news that happens close to home. We like to know what's going on in our own backyard, versus something that's happening in a faraway place. Local news is interesting and is most likely to have an impact on us personally or professionally.

One of the biggest pet peeves I hear from journalists who cover local news is when they receive press releases from people announcing an event that's happening in a town 500 miles away. This is an indication that the sender did a "spray and pray," which is sending the press release to every media outlet everywhere. It's spam, quite frankly.

"Proximity" is the low-hanging fruit of your publicity efforts, because your business will always have the advantage of being local.

David Meerman Scott coined the term, "newsjacking," which he defines as, "the art and science of injecting your ideas into a breaking news story to get media attention."

Timeliness

Being the first and fastest with a big, breaking news story is what every media outlet lives for. "New" is good, and the fresher, the better. If your story sits on the shelf too long, it gets stale. Give it to the media while it's hot, or it'll lose "love it" points.

We live in a 24/7 news cycle. That means that 24 hours from now, stories begin to age and wither. However, anything new that develops pertaining to that story can keep it alive for weeks, even months. Think of the O.J. Simpson trial, or the search for the black box after an airline crash, or the uncovering of new clues in a terrorist bombing incident.

Think of news as a loaf of fresh baked bread, or as fresh fruit sitting on your countertop. After a day or so, bread becomes stale and no one wants to eat it. A few days after that, your bread and fruit become moldy and what used to be delicious food is now completely unpalatable.

I recently consulted with a man who'd recently joined a company as CEO and wanted to announce his appointment with a press release. He knew he was well regarded in the industry and that many stakeholders would pay attention when they heard the news about him. Trouble was, he'd stepped into his new role more than six months previously. The opportunity to package his new, prestigious assignment as "news" had wilted on the vine. Instead, we introduced a major new initiative that the company had launched as a result of his leadership.

Keep the timeliness principle in mind as you brainstorm story ideas for you and your business. Are you launching something new this year? Are you going to form new strategic alliances, hire new people, move to a new location, or roll out a new product? All of these things are newsworthy in the eyes of the media.

Also, if a story breaks Wednesday afternoon that has relevance to your expertise and you wish to contribute insight to your media contacts, reach out to them immediately, that same day. Calling or emailing them the next day is too late. Then again, when a story breaks and they know you well, the odds are they'll call *you*. More about this later.

Consequence or Impact

The world is always changing, and as a species, humans are generally uncomfortable with change. Doesn't it seem like, just when we get used to something, and our life becomes predictable and worry-free, that BOOM! Something changes. And when something changes, there's usually some consequence, or impact, which could either be great and wonderful, or inconvenient and painful.

In crisis situations, people adopt the herd mentality, panic, and run for the fire exits. It's human nature to fear or resist what we do not know or understand. Traditionally, we've relied on an unbiased media to restore order by providing facts and information.

If something big is happening in your community or around the world, you don't usually pay a lot of attention to it unless something about it affects you personally. It's the media's job to let the community know when something is likely to have widespread impact.

The media keeps us informed about storm and flood warnings, tornado alerts, road closings, traffic backups, power outages, anything that's likely to affect many of us.

With the passing of the Homeland Security Act of 2002, many interesting story angles were presented by media outlets to help communicate the impact. Remember the passing of the Homeland Security Act that was introduced after the attacks on September 11? Its passing resulted in a general security lock-down on U.S. borders and air transportation and journalists told many stories about how people were affected.

I recall a photo of an 80-year-old woman who'd been asked to stand at an airport security station so that a TSA agent could pass his wand over the woman's body and wheelchair to search for deadly weapons. The photo did its job to convey that the increased security in airports would have very real consequences, and that no one was immune.

Are you someone who might be able to assist journalists by explaining what widespread consequences or impact a certain situation might have on your community, or nationally? For example, one of my clients, an expert in senior care, was interviewed by several media outlets to give advice on how seniors could prepare themselves when traveling by air.

As always, be cognizant of what's going on in the world and in the community, because you never know when your particular expertise is going to be useful to journalists whose duty is to inform and enlighten the public.

"Proximity" is the low hanging fruit of your publicity efforts, because your business will always have the advantage of being local.

Conflict and Controversy

If you're a writer, you know that the best stories need conflict to make them exciting. That's true whether you're writing fiction or a news story.

Earlier, I told you the story of an exciting confrontation at a small town city council meeting when community activists stormed the chambers to protest the building of a big box retailer in their neighborhood. "Not in my backyard (NIMBY)" protests always make for good storytelling.

Naturally, no one wants his business to be the focus of negative public opinion, and it's a good idea to have a crisis communications plan in place as a first aid kit in case of an emergency. (We'll cover ways to deal with a crisis in chapter 16.) There are situations, however, when you may be able to weigh in on controversial issues without risking harm to your reputation.

The editorial and op-ed sections of your local newspaper, for example, are always seeking opposing viewpoints or ideas on how to create positive change. Perhaps there's something going on in your industry that is dysfunctional or shortsighted? When the economy collapsed in 2008 and the banking industry faced new and crippling regulations, many experts stepped forward to voice their concerns and subject matter experts were in high demand.

Having a strong opinion on a divisive issue will always be in high demand from the media. If you have 'em, share 'em. Think of the pundits you know who appear regularly on TV to voice their unique perspectives on happenings specific to their expertise, e.g., the firing of a football coach, what's going to happen next as the result of a new regulation (the *impact*), your take on allowing teens to use their mobile phones at the dinner table, whether ageism exists in the hiring process, etc.

Your voice matters, and your opinions are valuable. Oliver Wendell Holmes famously said that, "the best test of truth is the power of an idea to get itself accepted in the competition of the market." Citizens of the United States are fortunate to enjoy the right of free speech, because free speech leads toward a universally accepted truth, and the truth, in the purest sense of journalism, struggles to prevail in the digital environment.

Scandal

A good scandal is almost guaranteed to be deemed newsworthy. Obviously, if you're in the public eye, avoid scandal at all costs. Look what happened to Lance Armstrong, Michael Milkin, Bill Cosby, Lindsay Lohan, Tiger Woods, companies who cheat their customers, writers who plagiarize, restaurants who appear on "Hotel Hell" and CEOs who drop the sacred ball of responsibility.

Once you're classified as a public figure, or have built a large following, all eyes are on you. With great power comes great responsibility. People, and the media, love to put heroes up on pedestals, and we flock like vultures on carrion when they topple to the ground.

As another point of clarification, public relations professionals do not exist solely to dig naughty clients out of bad situations. Our goal is to protect reputations and build positive brands, not sneak in when crisis hits to create messaging that rescues badly behaved corporations and prominent individuals. When we do our jobs right, adhering to a strict code of ethics, and you've committed a misdeed that creates negative public opinion, it is PR's duty to advise you to tell the truth and accept responsibility for your actions, and to make reparations when possible. A wise and wonderful mentor once taught me that integrity is the highest value of our profession, and accordingly, we must always take the high road.

Relevance

Every media outlet screens stories by asking, "Why does this matter?" or "Why would anyone care about this?" Seems obvious, right? Not so much, judging by the 300 or more emails the average editor gets every day that are completely irrelevant on a number of levels, i.e., wrong geography, wrong audience or self-serving promotional tripe.

Relevance is news that helps people make good decisions, grow personally or professionally, or learn how to build, do, or fix things. Your job is to be a resource to journalists. Gives them useful, relevant content, so that they, in turn, can serve their audiences.

Having a strong opinion on a divisive issue will always be in high demand from the media.

Human Interest

These are the stories that tug at our heartstrings, inspire, entertain, or are completely out of the ordinary. An instructor once told us that the media is attracted to stories of "beauties, beasts and babes," meaning celebrities, animals and children make for great human-interest stories.

When creating human-interest stories of your own, think in terms of superlatives: first, last, best, worst, biggest, smallest, or greatest. Strive to think of ways to tell your story and make people feel something. Remember, the heartstrings are connected to the purse strings. You'll see this concept played out when nonprofits and charities are in fundraising mode. Capture people's hearts, and you capture their wallets as well.

The human-interest stories you tell don't necessarily have to be tied to your industry or business. Put all of that commerce stuff aside and remember who you and your team are as people. Do you like wine? Race car driving? Travel? Baking? Charity work? If you wish (and it's an idea that works), your blog can be purely focused on the local music scene, even if you are an estate planning attorney, Realtor or life insurance salesman. People do business with you because they know, like and trust you, not because you sell life insurance.

Your business life abounds with human-interest stories, many of which will resonate with your media contacts.

David vs. Goliath

In the biblical tale of David and Goliath, the underdog, David, faced the challenge of hand-to-hand combat with an opponent who was much bigger than he was. People hid their eyes with their hands so they wouldn't have to watch David being beaten to a pulp. Instead, David faced his opponent with courage and determination and won the day.

People love stories of heroes who overcome incredible odds and triumph over their enemies, whether it be "the system," or a physical disability, or rising to entrepreneurial fame and fortune from the depths of poverty and despair.

Journalists often view their role as being the protector of the exploited, so in many cases, the "little guy" receives more sympathetic coverage than the person who appears to have all the advantages. Support the reporters in your town who are consumer advocates by helping them spot marketplace injustices, or by telling them stories of how you helped customers find justice or compassionate solutions.

Incompetence

You may have noticed that many of the central ideas of these news determinants run together. This one, "incompetence," is closely aligned with scandal, whereas a person in a position of great responsibility messes up by doing something foolish, illegal or disappointing.

When a corporate executive, sports figure, celebrity or politician messes up, the press pays big attention and the resulting public outcry is cruel and relentless. No one is perfect. If you ever find yourself in a position in which your good reputation is compromised because of a mistake or error in judgment, stand tall, accept responsibility, and move forward with integrity.

Surprise

Guess what! Experts say that some fat is actually good for you! Stories that contain an element of surprise are entertaining. Watch your nightly newscasts to spot how anchors incorporate an element of surprise to keep viewers engaged. "How did one local wine maker find buried pirate treasure?' says the anchor. "The answer might surprise you."

Hypocrisy

North Carolina Republican Senate candidate Steve Wiles campaigned heavily on his anti-gay beliefs and he strongly supported the state's same sex marriage ban. However, in May, 2014, news broke that just over a decade ago, he'd worked as an openly gay drag queen and drag-show emcee at a gay-friendly Winston-Salem lounge. Wiles also worked as a promoter for the 2011 Miss Gay America pageant.

The definition of hypocrisy is, "the practice of claiming to have moral standards or beliefs to which one's own behavior does not conform; pretense."

Again, public figures are held to higher standards of behavior and the media is always watching, holding to their commitment as watchdogs of the public good.

Take the Chapter 6 Quiz

Score 100 percent on every chapter quiz for your chance to win free tuition for the PR Breakthrough™ Publicity Boot Camp:

http://bit.ly/2gNscEk

Chapter 7

The Mighty Press Kit

"Information about the package is as important as the package itself."

— Frederick W. Smith

The "press kit" is a collection of useful content that helps journalists, investors and prospects find information about your business quickly and easily.

Let's say there's a reporter with a big story assignment and a tight deadline. She needs to find, by lunchtime, three community bank CEOs who will talk to her about the bank's policy on loan officers' use of LinkedIn as a business development tool.

She makes a list of three local community banks, and she visits each bank's website. The first thing she does is click on the "about us" button. She's looking for a succinct paragraph describing the organization and a list of key personnel with contact information. Unfortunately, many websites fail to provide content in the "about us" section that describes exactly what a company does, what it stands for and who runs it. If this essential information is missing, most reporters will leave your site.

However, this reporter decided to stick around and see if she could find an online press kit, because there she'll find exactly what information she needs, or at the very least (hopefully), the name, email address and phone number of a person who can put her immediately in touch with the CEO. Too typically, she does not find a press room button, and so, as a last resort, she will click on the "contact us" button. If there's nothing there but a contact form without a phone number, she'll leave the site.

If you hope to build a strong media relations program for your business, I urge you to provide a section on your website that is specially designed to help journalists get everything they need to prepare a story—company overview, contact information, biographies and more. The easier you make it for journalists to find the information they need to write their stories, the more likely it is that you'll garner trust and exposure. Remember, newsrooms are drastically understaffed these days and they need all the help they can get.

There are others who look at your press kit, too: potential customers, potential employees, potential investors, people who book speaking gigs and others who are interested in knowing about your company's real story without having to wade through all of the sales hype. Remember, your business has many audiences. If your website is nothing but a giant sales machine, you run the risk of missing out on other opportunities to build mutually beneficial relationships. If your website is a retail storefront, provide a link in the bottom navigation where reporters can locate corporate information.

Almost all press kits are online these days. They're very easy to find with a main navigation button labeled "newsroom," "press room" or just, "press." The content of the average press kit hasn't changed much over the years. Back in the day, a press kit was a pocket folder stuffed with documents, photos and audio CDs. They cost a small fortune to print, ship or mail. Reporters' offices were stacked high with them.

I'll describe the elements of a basic press kit in a moment, but first, I want to tell you what a press kit is *not*:

The "press kit" is a collection of useful content that helps journalists, investors and prospects find information about your business quickly and easily.

A press kit is *not* a "media kit." A media kit is a compilation of information that magazines put together to provide information to advertisers. It breaks down their demographics, how many readers they have, explains their philosophy, and provides ad sizes and pricing.

A press kit is *not* merely an archive of previous press coverage. If that's all that's in your press kit, it means that you've misunderstood the purpose and audience of a press kit. Don't worry. It's a common mistake, and you were partially right. It is nice to have clips of previous coverage in your press kit, if only to demonstrate that you are a competent media resource.

The press kit is *not* a "sales kit." You have plenty of opportunities to create sales demand with your marketing collaterals. Keep the audience for your press kit in mind— journalists, and perhaps people who have a vested interest in your company, such as investors or speaking agents. These folks are not interested in buying your products or services, only in knowing what they are and how they work. Their interest is to become familiar with you so that they can decide whether to write about you, interview you, book you, invest in you or work for you.

Press kits are often ***scenario dependent***. Because your press kit is a tool that assists journalists with the production of news stories, the purpose and contents of your press kit can vary. Some entities have several press kits. For an illustration of this, visit the NASA newsroom: http://www.nasa.gov/news/media/presskits/index.html. As you can see, every mission, project and initiative requires a different set of information components.

An organization with a booth at a trade show might create a general information press kit about the company and its offerings. A new product launch requires a press kit. If you're an author who seeks speaking engagements and media interviews, you could have a press kit that summarizes your work, or just your latest book release. In any case, your press kit should be available electronically and easily found on your web site. It should also be available as PDF downloads in the event you need to print out your press kit and take it with you to an event.

Following is a list of the items that are normally found in a press kit. Incidentally, I have enclosed samples of press documents and newsrooms in the Samples & Resources section.

Company Overview, or Corporate Backgrounder

This is a one-page, just-the-facts-ma'am description of your company. It explains what you do, how you got started, where you're located and other information that explains your reasons for existence. It's a succinct, well-written narrative; your organizational biography.

When I write press kits for my clients, I start with the overview page. This document lays out the foundation for many other pieces of content you will create to provide summary information on the business, e.g., boilerplate paragraphs for press releases (more on boilerplates later), "about us" descriptions, executive biographies, case studies, white papers and more.

My journalist friends tell me that the company overview is the first thing they read in a press kit. It's like reading the synopsis of a movie before deciding whether you want to see it. If the overview describes a company that is within their area of interest, they'll continue to browse the contents of your press kit.

Some people supplement the company backgrounder with other pieces of content that provide additional background about the company. Older companies that are decades old and steeped in tradition might include a *company history* or *timeline* page to drive home the point that they were founded in 1895 making horseshoes and today are one of the most recognized steel fabrication plants in the world.

As a reader of this book, you are welcome to join the Artful PR Community in Facebook. http://www.facebook.com/groups/ArtfulPRCommunity.

You are welcome to post your company backgrounder (and other press kit documents) and ask for feedback.

Biographies of Key Personnel

The very next section you should write is called "Biographies of Key Personnel." Companies who don't have biographies of their important personnel on their websites are really missing the boat. After all, it's the leadership and contingent of experts who make an organization attention worthy.

If you have already written a business plan, you've already written the biographies of the people who are essential to the management and function of your organization. If you don't have a business plan, now's your opportunity to add this key information to your "critical content" inventory. In addition to it being a key section of your press kit, it's also useful in new business proposals and RFPs.

Biographies of each person run an average of three to four paragraphs. Paragraph one describes that individual's function at the company. Paragraph two summarizes the person's previous experience, and paragraph three lists professional credentials, awards won and education. Paragraph four adds additional dimension to help readers get a feel for the individual's personality, such as hobbies, family, where they live, etc. Personally, I like biographies that present the subject as a well-rounded, likeable individual.

Include the biographies of the people who are in leadership positions. Journalists and investors like to know whether the organization is in capable hands. Also, include the biographies of anyone in the organization who is considered a "subject matter expert." These are people who are (or will be) media trained and articulate.

It's advisable to have a communications policy on file that specifies the process by which media interviews are conducted and through whom. Many of the clients I've worked with have teams that are sharp, charismatic, articulate and comfortable talking about the company with journalists. Some companies have staff members who are among the finest in their fields who need just a tad of training to help them bring their A games to journalists.

Another reason to have a communications policy is to ensure the right and best-qualified people are interacting with the media at all times. Perhaps you'd like for all media inquiries to go directly to the CEO, or to a dedicated in-house or outsourced PR representative. This policy will especially help you in times of crisis when reporters are scrambling for detailed information and need someone to talk to, fast. Make sure your employees know what your policy is and include it in their employee manual. There is more about crisis communications in a later chapter.

As a companion to the biographies of key personnel, offer high-resolution (300 dpi) headshots for download in your press kit. Offer the headshots as downloads. This is one of those helpful details that makes the journalist's job easier.

Frequently Asked Questions (FAQs)

Your aim with the FAQs is to answer the questions your ideal *client* or *ultimate end user* might have. Your task is to anticipate whatever questions you think a potential customer might ask, and answer them in the FAQ.

If you're an author or speaker, you may have a different approach to your FAQ. In this case, it's a good idea to produce a list of questions that a talk show interviewer might ask (which I label as "Interview Questions.") Every FAQ should answer the who, what, when, where, why and how, and any other questions your audience might have.

Examples of questions are: How much are tickets? What do they cost? Where do I buy them? Is the event open to the public? What's your book about? What is the purpose of this event? Why did you create this product? What is the audience for your book/product/event? Where do I go for additional information? Who are the event organizers? Who benefits from the proceeds of this event? There are samples of FAQs in the "resource" section of this book.

Fact Sheet

The fact sheet is a bulleted list that calls out or summarizes important items of information that makes your news item, announcement or event newsworthy. It's a good place to list facts and statistics from third party sources, with citations. It indicates to the journalist that your claims are valid, but more importantly, you help the journalist by having done some supportive research. Your diligence saves the reporter time and effort.

For example, if you were launching a mobile app that helps people who have been affected by a cancer diagnosis,[9] you would want to search the Internet and find facts and statistics about cancer diagnoses. The fact sheet is also a place to list some interesting facts about your company, industry and marketplace. It's a way to demonstrate to journalists that your story is newsworthy by showing relevance, human interest or proximity (e.g., more than 50,000 people were diagnosed with cancer in [your community name] last year.)

The press kit is meant to be a helpful resource to journalists who are writing a story about you or your industry, and every document you include should be with that aim in mind. Reporters are almost always on deadline and they don't have nearly as much time as they'd like to do the research they need to do to get accurate facts and statistics.

Don't forget to include facts that are notable about your own product or service. If you are the first to do something, say so, and if you are the biggest or first to market, point that out. (Back up your claims with verifiable facts whenever possible.)

This is not the place for pricing or ordering information. Instead, provide this information in your press release and FAQs.

Logos, Images, Graphics and Video

Have all of these items available in several formats for easy download. The easier it is to find and download your high quality logo or image, the

9 Fact sheet example: http://www.cansurround.com

more likely it will be used. Include high-resolution photos of products, locations and historic events.

Having a logo online and available for download is a good move. Every company ought to have a set of "graphic design standards" to ensure other people are using your logo correctly.

It's a best practice in the digital age to help journalists illustrate your story with pictures and video. Be sure to provide high resolution head shots of your key personnel and spokespersons.

Be creative, and exhaustive. Think through what images you can provide that will help the journalist's audience wrap their heads around whatever it is you're describing in your press kit. Sometimes, a media outlet will prefer to shoot its own video or pictures, but not always. Mark Eichmann, who produces a weekly television news magazine for WHYY in Delaware, says there are (rare) times when video shot by others has been useful. For example, there was a story about an increase in the coyote population in the region. An attentive viewer, who was a deer hunter perched silently on a tree branch, managed to capture video footage of a coyote as it crept below him. He posted it on YouTube, and WHYY used it for their news segment.

Product Demonstrations and Reviews

The press kit for a product launch might include a way for journalists to experience your product or service for themselves so that they can write a review of it. Remember when I told you I had once been an "experiential journalist?" My job was to write about new products or services by experiencing them firsthand. Each company's press kit included carefully detailed instructions on how the media outlet could take advantage of the demo.

In several cases, the company included a sample of the product with the press kit. I sampled weighted jump ropes, inline skates, free training, nutritional supplements and bicycle seats.

An Arizona-based start-up company launched a new technology that was a "first-to-market" solution for converting paper into digital filing and storage. Its press kit, sent exclusively to technology sector product reviewers, provided journalists with everything they needed to experience the product: login IDs, passwords, and a limited supply of bar-coded Post-it Notes developed in partnership with 3M. Our team thought this through to the minutest detail, including having on hand a dedicated product specialist to troubleshoot issues and conduct live online walk-throughs for journalists. The product launch was a huge success and garnered coverage in some of the leading technology publications.

In the "old days," we used to plan multi-city tours to visit the major media outlets with the hope of being able to demonstrate our products in person or schedule appearances on local television and radio stations. I'll talk more about this in chapter 14, when I talk about press tours.

White Papers

Having a white paper is not an essential element of your product launch press kit, but it makes you look good if you have one. A white paper is an educational piece that is helpful to industry and trade media, corporate decision makers and your ultimate end users. It establishes your thought leadership, credibility and subject matter expertise. The media likes having experts on tap to help them with source material and interview subjects. Additionally, a white paper has foundational verbiage you can use to create numerous other marketing pieces, such as fact sheets, FAQs, brochures, contributed articles, presentations, videos and website content.

We'll talk a lot more about white papers in Chapter 9. The point of including it here is to emphasize that the more you can establish your subject matter expertise in your press kit, the better your chances to attract media attention. Companies who have a library of white papers often create an archive for them on their websites.

Press Release Archive

Each time you issue a press release, publish it in your online newsroom. There are a couple of benefits to doing this. One is that it does wonders for your Search Engine Optimization (SEO). Web crawlers continually search for new content and keyword-rich text. Second, journalists (and other key publics) have the option of reading through previous press releases, thus further reassuring themselves of your credibility.

However, do not make your press release archive the sole content of your online newsroom. It's irritating to journalists if they go to the newsroom expecting to find a professional press kit.

Previous Press Coverage

There are a few circumstances (and only a few) when journalists are interested in reading your previous press coverage. For instance, if you've been interviewed on radio or television before and have video and audio clips, then producers who are considering you for talk shows or other segments can watch to see how well you perform on camera or in front of a microphone. If you've scored feature articles about yourself or any of the key personnel profiled in your press kit, having these articles available for viewing go another step in building up your "celebrity" factor. Remember "prominence" as a news determinant? Having clips gives the impression that you have an audience. NOTE: Include only *important* news clips in this section, the ones where the media outlet singled you out for coverage.

Take the Chapter 7 Quiz

Score 100 percent on every chapter quiz for your chance to win free tuition for the PR Breakthrough™ Publicity Boot Camp:

http://bit.ly/2gebj5Q

Chapter 8

Selling Your Story: The Pitch and the Press Release

"If you don't take your audience seriously, you can be sure it will return the favor."

— *Billy Marshall Stoneking*

There are rules for most things in life, and it's up to you as a well branded professional to know what the protocols are in any given situation. My mother used to insist that we speak the English language properly and to comport ourselves elegantly at the dinner table. We learned the socially correct ways of doing things so that we'd be able to handle ourselves according to the dictates of our surroundings, a.k.a., the *appropriate* use of language. If everyone else at the dinner table is using their fingers to eat chicken or has their elbows on the table, it's okay if you do, too. Sometimes, it's about fitting in.

The risk takers and world shakers amongst us say that rules are made to be broken, and in the business world, this is often true. A very successful music publicist I know, Randy Alexander, says that there are no rules in publicity. I'm inclined to agree. Just when you believe you're doing things the right way, someone else steps up and does the unexpected, breaks the mold, ignites the collective imagination and inspires copycat behavior.

Back in the days when my dream was to become a famous songwriter, the challenge was to get one's demo tape into the hands of the big record companies or anyone else who could have a significant, positive impact on my songwriting career. The next step was to get them to actually listen to the demo, but that's a moot point if they didn't get it in the first place. I read every songwriter magazine I could get my hands on to find out who the industry influencers were. My favorite articles were stories about the successful songwriters who had broken the rules to get the attention of their idols and the important dealmakers by doing outrageous, courageous things.

One story was about how actor and songwriter Kris Kristofferson, then young, and struggling, landed a National Guard helicopter on Johnny Cash's lawn and stepped out of it with his demo tape in one hand and a cold beer in the other. (This later turned out to be more fact than fiction.) Kris was living in a low rent apartment at the time and was so committed to becoming a songwriter that rather than accept a professorship at the U.S. Military Academy, he swept floors at Columbia Studios, waiting for his big break. Other now-famous singers and songwriters drove from city to city in old, beat-up cars to hand deliver their demo tapes to radio disc jockeys and plead for airplay.

First, you need to know the rules.
Then, you need to know when to break them.

The same principles held true for getting press kits into the hands of influential journalists and broadcast producers. The "proper" way of sending a press kit was to send it through the mail in a large manila envelope. Hundreds of press kits were delivered to newsrooms every week, and offices were piled high with unopened, plain vanilla manila envelopes, many of which eventually landed in the dumpster out back.

Publicists, though, are creative people by nature, and they found many ways to break the rules, doing all kinds of original things to compel journalists to open their press kits. Press kits arrived in long tubes or uniquely shaped boxes. They were delivered by messengers dressed as apes or from window washers suspended outside their skyrise offices. Some publicists sent singing telegrams or people dressed as police officers. The idea was, of course, to separate your press kit from the hundreds of others and entice the recipients to open them.

The challenge of getting people to open and read your email is universal to all businesses, is it not? The quest for attention in today's electronic age is no different than it was in the bygone days of direct mail and courier service. It has always been a matter of "cutting through the clutter" to get your message noticed, opened and acted upon. There are hundreds, maybe thousands, of competitors out there, all of whom are chasing the same audiences as you, and many of whom are 10 times more clever, persistent and well financed than you are.

Fear not. It's an abundant universe with plenty to go around if you're passionate, professional, prepared, patient and original. First, you need to know the rules. Then, you need to know when to break them. But always, you need to have the goods, which is a newsworthy story or event. Without it, you're just an annoying interruption in an ape costume.

First, what are the so-called rules? Most of the journalists I've talked to say that they prefer to be approached with requests for coverage or story ideas via email. Snail mail, they claim, is a thing of the past, and phone calls, they say, are obtrusive and a nuisance. When you and a journalist have developed a pleasant working relationship, there won't be such stringent requirements on the method of contact, but in those early, dark times when you're going in as a stranger, the best bet is to give your media contacts what they say they want. My recommendation is that all of your initial contact be by email unless your news is undeniably earth shaking.

There are two primary pieces of communication that you use to tell journalists about your newsworthy story or event: the "press release" and the "pitch." But before you do any of that, I recommend that you send a short letter of introduction introducing yourself and letting them know that you're going to enjoy being one of their valuable resources in the years to come. We'll talk more about making introductions in Chapter 11 when I explain the relationship building process.

Press Release

The press release is a news story written in AP style and packaged according to customs established in the early years of print publishing. Following the proper format shows that you are a trained PR professional who is sensitive to the needs of the journalist receiving it, in the way that knowing which fork to use at a formal dinner party demonstrates to the hostess she made the right decision inviting you to her table. No one likes to be thought of as a barbarian, or a cretin, or someone who didn't go to the trouble to learn how to do it the right way.

Writing a simple news story was one of the first skills we honed in journalism school. It took loads of practice to get it right. There are many details and rules of grammar to learn. Failure to comply with these rules results in a failing grade at school and in the newsroom.

Construction of the news story is paramount. The essence of the story and all of the most important facts are relayed immediately, in the first paragraph, in 45 words or less. This is called the "lead" paragraph, and it took me weeks to get it right. The model for the structure of a news story is the "news pyramid," with the short lead paragraph at the top, a bit more information in the second paragraph, a bit more in the third, and so on.

In the lead paragraph, include who, what, when, where, why and how. By reading this paragraph, readers have all of the information they need to know about the story. If they want more details and insight, they read more.

The order of the words you use in the lead paragraph are often a dead giveaway of whether you've been trained as a journalist. "Five were killed Tuesday and three others injured when a passenger van collided with a loaded semi truck on the Walt Whitman Bridge, said police." "When" follows the verb. For some reason, many of our writing assignments were about auto accidents and remembering to use the word, "alleged" in crime stories.

You can also spot a non-trained press release writer by the way they attribute quotes. The right way is, "We are very pleased that Jane has joined our company," said John Smith, president and CEO. An untrained writer might write, "John Smith commented as follows: 'We are very pleased that Jane has joined our company.'" Also, an amateur will not have used the AP Stylebook to ensure that job titles and other non-proper nouns are not capitalized.

Most of the press releases I write average five paragraphs. The first, of course, is the ***lead paragraph***, 45 words or less. ***Paragraph two*** elaborates a bit more on the lead paragraph, giving a bit more detail. ***Paragraph three*** is usually a quote from a source who is an authority on the matter or in a top leadership position. ***Paragraph four***, typically, explains to the reader what actions he/she needs to take, an explanation of what's going to happen next, or where the reader can go to find more details. At the end of the release is a boilerplate paragraph, explained in the next section.

Formatting

In the upper left corner of your press release are the words, ***"For Immediate Release."*** This tells the media outlet that they can use the information immediately. In some rare cases, people will put ***"For Release on [Date],"*** meaning the news in the press release shouldn't be published until that date. You might do this if you have a big product launch coming up, and you'd like media outlets not to print your announcement until the day your product hits the market.

Beneath "For Immediate Release," include ***contact information*** of the person to call or email should the media outlet have questions or a need for additional information. Make sure this contact person is available 24/7 to take media calls. I always give them my cell phone number.

I have heard many horror stories from journalist friends who weren't able to reach the person listed as the contact on the press release. For example, one journalist got lost on the way to covering an event and wasn't able to reach the contact person by phone. Once you've gone A.W.O.L. on a reporter who's been assigned to cover your story, you will never recover that person's complete trust.

There have been times when a client will insist that he/she be listed as the media contact person on a press release. More than once, they haven't been around when the journalist needed them. These days, if a client asks to be listed as the contact, I make them double-dog swear they'll have their cell phone turned on and on their person at all times after the press release has been sent out.

Make sure the contact is prepared to answer all of the reporter's questions, and that they have the authority to do so. If they don't have knowledge or authority, it just slows things down. If the CEO is the only person qualified to speak on a matter to the press, then the CEO should be listed as the contact person on the press release, or promise to be available when a journalist calls.

If you are the designated public relations person and it's mandated by the boss that your name goes on press releases as the official contact person, and/or you've been assigned the role of "liaison" between the press and the official spokespersons in your organization, then you must arrange to have 24/7 access to all of the people who are qualified to respond to media inquiries. You must have all of their cell phone numbers and email addresses, and then make them commit to being available within a moment's notice if a reporter needs to speak with them. The turnaround time for responding to a journalist's call for information is about 10 seconds. Don't make them wait. They're on deadline, but even more important, if you don't help, there are plenty of competitors who will. Worse, the spurned reporter may put you on his "black list."

The ***headline*** is centered at the top of the release, after the contact information. Keep it as brief as you can. Back in the old days, our headlines had to fit within the column width. The aim of the headline is to tell the entire story in as few characters as possible, as we've learned to do with our Twitter posts.

Before your lead paragraph starts, you must include the "***dateline***." This orients the reader by telling her where and when the story originated.

At the end of your press release, you will add the ***boilerplate*** paragraph. The boilerplate always says the same thing. The term boilerplate originated in the printing industry circa early 1900s.[10] It's a summary of the entity that is sending the press release, or, a one-paragraph description of your company and its products or services. Typically, the boilerplate contains the same information that's in the first paragraph of your company overview. The last sentence in the boilerplate says, "For additional information, visit [website address] or call [phone number].

There is a press release template for your reference in the Samples & Resources section.

The Pitch

Also called a "query letter," the pitch is an email asking an editor if they're interested in your story idea, or whether they can spare the resources to cover your event. One of your challenges is getting someone who doesn't know you to open and read your email. A few decades ago, we used to send non-time-sensitive pitch letters through the regular mail, which may, or may not, have been opened by recipients. People would do what they could to get noticed, like use scented paper or bright orange envelopes, but it was still a crapshoot because of the sheer volume of mail editors received every day. Similarly, editors' phones rang off the hook all day, every day, and if they picked up the phone, if just to stop the noise, they sounded gruff and irritated to the person on the other end of the line. It was a tough job—calling those busy newsrooms.

The invention of the fax machine gave PR people a whole new way to pummel the newsroom with pitches. However, the fax gave the sender a

10 https://en.wikipedia.org/wiki/Boilerplate_(text)

new advantage: the "memorandum" format, which allowed the sender to use a subject line. Rather than having to slit open an envelope and pull out the contents to determine the sender's intentions, or having to pick up the phone and have one's time wasted by someone babbling nonsense on the other end, the editor could now read a fax subject line and make an immediate decision of whether to keep or toss.

As of this writing, most pitches should be sent via email and formatted as follows:

The ***subject line*** remains the most crucial section of every email communication, regardless of with whom you're attempting to communicate. It has to be interesting, relevant or from someone they know, or the intended recipient will delete it without reading. It's nothing personal. There's just too much information out there, and too much of it is irrelevant.

In Chapter 11, "Making Contact," we're going to learn how to be one of those people whose emails are opened. Becoming a trusted insider is the holy grail of artful PR. When you're starting out fresh with a new media contact, however, the priority becomes how to write a subject line that will get your email opened and read.

It's okay to be clever and cheeky. It's perfect to be tantalizing. It's best, though, to just get to the damn point, while we're all young. *Teenage Girl Wins Nobel Peace Prize... Local Community Bank Names New CEO... Carrots Make You Fat, Doctor Claims... Governor to Appear at Ground Breaking Ceremony on Thursday... New Law Mandates Pay Equity for Women*—(Sound of needle scraping on vinyl record.)

You get the idea. It's not always vital to have a subject line that's so intriguing that even Ebenezer Scrooge[11] would open it, but if your pitch is apropos to the person or media outlet to whom you've sent it, make it known in the subject line. Media outlets are always, always, always looking for good, relevant content.

Format your pitch as you would any professional correspondence:

11 https://youtu.be/dYHmQT_7a2c

Dear Frank:

This first paragraph tells you immediately that my story idea is relevant to your audience. I'm going to make a provocative statement, or share a surprising fact, perhaps mention that I've read or seen your previous pieces on the subject matter I'm about to present. In this way, you'll know I've done my homework and have taken the trouble to familiarize myself with your work. It's important to me that you think this idea is relevant and worth pursuing. This is my way of showing respect.

This second paragraph will explain the impact of what I've told you in the first paragraph. It will reel out several more facts, or tell you the brief story of how this situation came to be. It might also make the case that this story is pertinent to your readers.

Now I'm going to tell you how I can be of service to you to put this story together. I can deliver people to interview and assure you the process will run smoothly, or I'll give you a press pass, sign you up for a demo, or anything else that will make your life easier.

To wrap up, I'm going to ask something like, "Is this something you might be interested in?" I'm happy to answer questions or provide additional information. My number is (102) 345-6789.

That's your basic pitch letter. Short, to the point, relevant and with clear instructions on how to get in touch with you.

Which One? The Pitch or the Press Release?

The ***press release*** is a vehicle for mass transmission, when it's necessary (or advantageous) to reach out to all of the pertinent outlets on your media list at the same time.

Publicly owned companies, for example, are required by the Securities and Exchange Commission (SEC) to provide "timely financial disclosure" whenever they release financial results, or when an event is likely to have an effect on share prices. The rule was made to prevent any unfair advantages to people who have access to inside information. Public companies must do their best to get the word out to as many outlets as possible, particularly the outlets that distribute financial information, to demonstrate compliance.

If the CEO is the only person qualified to speak On a matter to the press, then the CEO should be listed as the contact person on the press release, or at least, agree to be available if a journalist calls.

Media outlets "pick up" press releases all the time, especially if they're written as complete news stories. There's always a need for good content, and local publications in particular are warm to press releases they can simply plug into open slots.

A press release is an announcement. If you're holding an event, many outlets will print the details in their "calendar of events" section. If you're announcing that someone got hired or promoted, your release may appear in the "new hires/promotions" section. If you're announcing a new product or service, it's okay to send out a press release, but if you're hoping for more in-depth coverage, it's better to send a pitch letter.

With the ***pitch***, you communicate with one journalist at a time. It's a targeted, personalized, one-on-one conversation with someone to interest them in writing, or producing, a story about you or the subject matter you've proposed.

Media outlets all have their own particular brands and styles. They like to make "discoveries," and present unique angles. If it's an important story, they want to be the ones to cover it and not feel as though they've been mass marketed to. I like to offer "exclusives" to the most influential media outlets. With an exclusive, you promise your contact that you will not pitch the story to anyone else if they will agree to cover it. It's a win-win, i.e., it's a gift to the journalist, and a more important story for you.

By sending your press release, you've indicated to journalists that you have sent the same information to many other media outlets. That's okay. They may still want to pursue the story, especially if it has extraordinary newsworthiness.

Take the Chapter 8 Quiz

Score 100 percent on every chapter quiz for your chance to win free tuition for the PR Breakthrough™ Publicity Boot Camp:

http://bit.ly/2fmxOD8

Chapter 9

Content: Releasing the Kracken

"There's not much point in spinning a yarn if your audience keeps losing the thread."

— P.K. Shaw

The idea of using content strategically to generate awareness isn't new, but the internet's potential to reach the attention of millions at low or no cost has turned on the fire hose, and it's time for you to get in the game and think more deeply about content. It's the difference between your connecting meaningfully with your audiences versus merely treading water in a vast sea of unimaginative, self-serving babble. The cream always rises to the top.

If publicity is the extension of your brand message via the media armada, then content is the keeper of the flame, or the ocean upon which your business ship floats.

Content is anything that expresses or conveys the character or essence of something. It is information delivered through any channel that can be perceived by the senses: the written word, speech, images, audio, music, video, art, performance, television, food, fashion, braille, Morse code—any way a message can be communicated. Content is the substance, and the medium is the vehicle.

In his book, "Understanding Media: The Extensions of Man,"[12] media analyst Marshall McLuhan famously said, "The medium is the message," which means that how a message is transmitted affects how that message is perceived. In other words, if a message is scrawled on a wall as graffiti, it will be interpreted differently in the mind of the viewer than if those words had appeared in a scholarly journal. It's an important principle, and it plays a large role in how we produce content for our target audiences.

PR has always been about establishing mutually beneficial relationships with target publics, so the term, "audience engagement," looms large in all of the public relations programs and publicity campaigns you create. No matter what your business is about, what products you manufacture, what services you provide, none of it matters unless you're serving and pleasing your audience with good content. This should seem obvious, but there are many, many stories of businesses that failed because they forgot they were in business to provide education, information and value.

I learned this lesson the hard way, and ironically, I learned it during a sold-out performance. Our band, Dobson & Dobson, had been booked as the opening act for David Brenner at The Broadway Theatre of Pitman, New Jersey. His performances usually sold out, and I was particularly thrilled because it meant I could showcase some of my best original tunes. Fame was on the horizon. I could *smell* it!

...think more deeply about content. It's the difference between your connecting meaningfully with your audience versus merely treading water in a vast sea of unimaginative, self-serving babble. The cream always rises to the top.

So, there we were, on stage, looking great, singing our little hearts out, the band as tight as ever, and though the audience applauded politely after

12 Originally published in 1954 by Mentor, New York; reissued 1994, MIT Press, Cambridge, Massachusetts with an introduction by Lewis Lapham

each of my original tunes, it was clear we weren't bringing down the house. I kept thinking of Milton Berle's line, "What is this, an audience, or an oil painting?"

Toward the end of our set, we performed our version of "The Rose," a ballad that had been made famous by Bette Midler and was very popular at the time. When the song was finished, we got a standing ovation. We ended the set there. Better to leave the stage with the audience on its feet than risk another round of golf claps after one of my original tunes. (Also, in the middle of the set, we'd attempted to perform Natalie Cole's big hit, "This Will Be," and it was so awful and embarrassing that I'm reluctant to talk about it to this day outside of therapy, and only then after a few glasses of wine.

My lesson was this: the audience responded to "The Rose" because the song was familiar to them. They'd heard it before, and it was beloved in the popular culture. It was the type of tune that people in their demographic wanted to hear. My songs were unknown to them, having not yet made it to the mainstream. It's the dreary reality of a struggling unknown performing artist, that people will not respond to you at first, because you have not yet made yourself familiar to them with your content.

As a side note, the universal advice to anyone who's struggling is to not give up. When you're just starting out, the world appears a vast, impenetrable wall of exclusion, cruelty and disinterest. I've seen the most talented people languishing outside of this wall, throwing themselves against it in despair, year after year, out of money and broken hearted. The struggle is to keep going until people, who are essentially herd animals, become familiar with you, because you're out there regularly, doing it again, and again, and again. If you truly have the talent, keep going.

What Dobson & Dobson had done, then, by playing mostly my original tunes, was give the audience something that *we* wanted, and not what *they* wanted. It didn't matter how good or catchy my songs were, or how well the band played. We were a bunch of unknown, young musicians playing rock music in an auditorium filled with David Brenner fans who, had we done a little research, skewed older and preferred more sedate, middle-of-the-road, top-40 music. We ought to have taken that into consideration. We failed to please the audience.

Content,[13] then, must be planned and prepared with the audience in mind. Your audience wants messaging it can relate to, understand and appreciate, in a form that's appropriate for the message and that has context for their lives. Content must be the articulation of your corporate soul, infused with your unique voice, deep expertise and in the spirit of service to the receiver. Content is not for you. It's for *them.*

Content is not limited to the written word. Content is the means of exchange between you and the audiences you serve, packaged and delivered in unique ways depending on the context of the message. It is proactive and meaningful, requiring a personal touch.

Edu Marketing

Edu-Marketing is a relatively new term in the marketing world. It's a turn of phrase that expresses what the public relations function has been doing all along.

Traditional marketing is concerned with selling products and services to the ultimate end-user and purchase influencers. Marketing content (print ads, TV and radio commercials, brochures, direct mail, squeeze pages, etc.) is produced by people known as "copywriters," who are master manipulators of human behavior. A skilled copywriter can make you want *anything*. It's an incredible talent, and they deserve the big bucks they get paid.

Since the digital age, however, marketers are having to rethink how they communicate their sales messages, because the flow of information has become so rampant that people are becoming immune to advertising. Nowadays, we can fast forward through commercials, watch commercial free programming and tune out anything else that's not immediate or relevant. And so, marketers are scrambling to re-invent themselves to engage customers in a whole different way—without selling right out of

13 In this book, we're talking about "content" in the purely commercial sense. If you seek profit and prestige, you must give the people holding the purse strings what they want. To those of you who create art (painting, sculpting, composing, dance), plug your ears.

the gate. Some copywriters find this extremely difficult to understand. Why produce *any* content that doesn't ask for the sale? You might as well be asking them to describe a spiral staircase without using their hands.

Content must be planned and prepared with the audience (not you) in mind.

As a result, the lines between marketing copy and public relations content have started to blur, because marketing is trying to adopt the same methods of communication and audience engagement that public relations practitioners have been doing all along.

PR has always been about stimulating meaningful conversations with the outside world by engaging in two-way communication. PR uses content to facilitate the creation of these conversations.

You know why so many people are failing to see business results with their social media? It's because they're not engaging their audience. They're cramming themselves into an over-crowded digital space. They're paying someone to go in there and pump out agenda-laden content, and lots of it. But you know why it's called "social" media? It's to be social, to connect, to engage in conversation, to form mutually beneficial, or enjoyable relationships. Social media is a participatory sport, or ballroom dancing, without physical touch. Pick one channel, or two, but only if your audience is in there, and invite people to dance.

There are two types of educational documents that are must-haves in your public relations content arsenal: white papers and case studies.

The White Paper

The white paper is one of the most powerful tools you can have in your edu-marketing arsenal for a number of reasons. It proves you are an expert and an industry leader. It's one of the best ways to attract qualified leads to your business or grow your mailing list. This versatile document earns the trust of your target audiences and can be used in a multitude of ways.

There are thousands of people who are interested in your area of expertise, no matter how narrowly niched you are. If you can learn to harness the knowledge that's inside your head and express it in written form, you will have the power to market your ideas much more broadly than you ever thought possible.

White papers have been around for ages, first as political documents to explain issues, and later by the technology industry to explain to engineers (in complicated, esoteric language only the propeller heads could understand) how something worked. The white paper has entered the mainstream and is far less complicated than it used to be, but still, it is a particular style of document that follows a strict protocol in terms of how information is organized and presented.

White papers may be written for virtually any type of entity: banks, landscapers, coaching, beauty salons, real estate, health care, law—you name it. All you need is a topic that captures the attention of the audience for which it was intended.

According to white paper expert Michael Stelzner[14], a well-written white paper:

* Begins by addressing a problem, challenge or need, rather than the solution, which is presented at the end.
* Ranges from five to 12 pages in length, on average, at most.
* Educates readers as its highest priority.
* Avoids direct selling; it is NOT a sales piece.
* Focuses on benefits more than features.
* Contains information useful to the reader.
* Avoids the use of humor.

The white paper typically targets key decision makers and presents information that educates and persuades the reader. "How-to" papers are

14 Stelzner, Michael A. (2007), "Writing White Papers: How to Capture Readers and Keep Them Engaged." WhitePaperSource Publishing: Poway, CA.

especially popular, as are educational papers and papers that present and explain survey or research results.

The more you understand your target audience, the more effective and useful your white paper will be. The goal is to address a specific problem or challenge your target audience is facing, or to present deeper insight into the topic in which your readers are interested.

I'm somewhat of a white paper junkie, not just professionally, but personally, too. I'm always downloading white papers that will help me sharpen my public relations, writing, digital marketing and speaking skills. One of my habits is to print them out and add them to the pile of "stuff to read later" on my bedside table. White papers, especially the "how-to" ones, give me actionable information that I can implement almost immediately.

White papers have numerous advantages. For one thing, a white paper is ***likely to be shared with others.*** According to MarketingSherpa.com, 69 percent of prospects who download and like your white paper will actively pass it along to other interested parties, and 36 percent of total downloads will be passed on to a supervisor. White papers have a long shelf life, too, so the leads from one paper often trickle in for weeks or months after it's first published.

The white paper typically targets key decision makers and presents information that educates and persuades the reader.

White papers also ***generate lots of leads***. The most popular way to capture leads with your white paper is to use it as a lead magnet and offer it to your audience as a free download or special bonus from your website or landing page. Readers register for the download by providing basic contact information such as first name and email address.

By the time you've finished researching and writing your white paper, you'll have much of the foundational verbiage you can use to create ***numerous other marketing pieces***, such as fact sheets, FAQs, brochures, contributed articles presentations, videos and website content.

White papers ***establish your expertise and thought leadership***. You become an authority on your topic. When it's time for your prospect to make a decision, they'll remember you, who took the initiative to propose solutions to their most pressing concerns.

White papers help you ***earn trust in the eyes of potential customers***. Your poor target audience is pounded daily by marketing messages from businesses whose products or services they don't need or want. We've become so saturated, overdosed and assaulted by companies that sometimes you probably find yourself "talking to the hand" or a dial tone before you even have a chance to open your mouth. It's hard to break through.

Your white paper, however, does not sell—it educates. It informs. It explains things. It teaches readers how to do something. It offers solutions. And so, your willingness to share without a blatant agenda or ramming your product down the readers' throats earns their trust.

White papers ***help key decision makers and influencers make their case for implementing solutions***. In the corporate sector, line and staff managers must justify large purchases by conducting extensive due diligence and research. This is especially true with the adoption of new, enterprise-wide technology initiatives. Your white paper is an invaluable tool for demonstrating your particular understanding of the problem at hand. In smaller businesses, the challenge is more about generating awareness and trust of your expertise to consumers on the verge of making purchase decisions.

It's a reality that, more often than not, our message doesn't get through to the intended recipient because there are people in between preventing it. These are the gatekeepers. The beauty of a white paper is that ***it bypasses the gatekeepers***. Gatekeepers have little control over blocking your white paper because the document enters the business or household by the permission of the people who download them from their own computers.

White papers help you ***close sales***. The more people who read your white paper, the better your chance of closing a deal. MarketingSherpa.

com[15] says that 57 percent of IT purchase decision makers say a white paper influenced at least one buying decision in the past 12 months.

A typical white paper gets liked, re-tweeted, passed along or even becomes viral. It ***creates buzz around your new product or service.*** If you touch a chord in a member of your potential fan base, "sharing" happens. And, if your target media outlets find your white paper interesting, you may be chosen for an article or interview.

If you're looking to ***land speaking engagements***, then having a white paper or two is an advantage. There are hundreds of groups out there who book speakers with expertise like yours. Use your white paper as part of your speaking package. Use your white paper as the foundation for a TED talk! That is, if your white paper contains an, "idea worth spreading."

A white paper ***educates your customers and prospects***. Suppose you're a landscaper who specializes in ecologically friendly gardening techniques. You could write a white paper about, "10 Effective Ways to Eliminate Weeds the Natural Way." Are you a house painter? "The Secrets of Paint Prep Used by Experts." A home stager? "Before and After: How Clearing Clutter Gets Your Home Sold Faster." These examples are simplistic, but in each case, you've addressed situations that are likely to occur for people when they're in "buying mode" for a professional like you.

Many companies use white papers as ***training tools for new employees***. With a single document, employees develop a clear understanding of your brand and gain the ability to articulate your messages to customers and prospects. Employees also gain a sense of pride, knowing they are working for a business that is run by forward thinkers and industry influencers.

Last, but not least, a white paper is a phenomenal way to ***garner media coverage***. You will pitch it to relevant media outlet and include it in your press kit, of course, and since it's a solid foundation piece, your white paper can be the basis for guest appearances on radio shows and podcasts.

15 http://www.marketingsherpa.com/article/how-to/how-to-syndicate-your-white2

White Paper Rules of Thumb

Do you have a long sales cycle? As a PR consultant, trainer and coach, I do a lot of work in the corporate sector, and I've waited for up to two years before a client makes the decision to work with me. I work in a crowded profession. What helps me stay in the game during that long period of time until the potential client finally decides to pull the trigger is the fact that I made a powerful first impression with one of my white papers and loads of frequent, valuable content.

The white paper is NOT a sales piece. That is not the intention of a white paper at all. A white paper is meant to educate. Nothing turns the reader off faster than realizing as they're reading your white paper that you're only trying to sell them something, at which point they'll throw down your so-called white paper in disgust. If you're that desperate to sell, consider writing a long form sales letter instead. Don't try and disguise it as a white paper. You'll lose major credibility points.

A white paper starts by talking about a problem that people or businesses have, and proposes a solution to that problem after you have provided some well-researched analysis of the problem and how people have tried to solve it in the past. If you have a product or service that solves the problem, you want to talk about the benefits of your solution, not the features.

This is an academic document. Don't attempt to be cute or funny. A white paper is to be taken seriously. If you want to be cute, write an article or eBook or make it the style of your blog. An audience member once asked me, "What if it's your business to be funny?" That's a fair question. No matter how you slice it, a white paper is a serious, academic document. If you want to write a white paper, I answered, consider educating people about "funny" and why it's important. Back up your claims with solid evidence. It's out there! There's plenty of data to suggest humor does wonders for the human spirit.

If the idea of writing a white paper sounds laborious and time consuming, you're right. This isn't a document that you will write overnight. If you do it right, expect your white paper project to take at least six to eight weeks for a first draft. But believe me, you will be rewarded for your effort.

The 3 30 3 Rule

This rule was developed after extensive research of human behavior and communications by Clay Schoenfeld[16] and how we react to written information the first time we see it. It's science. Your white paper, and everything else you write, needs to grab the reader's attention right away. The rule goes like this:

* You have three seconds to grab the reader's attention. If you don't, they're gone, and you won't get a second chance.
* If you make it past three seconds, the reader will give you 30 more seconds, but that's it. Those 30 seconds are crucial.
* If you make it past 30 seconds, the reader will give you another three minutes, at least. If you've done a great job and your material is relevant and interesting, the reader may stick around to the end of your piece.

One of the great ways to keep your readers sticking around is to include interesting graphics to break up the text. Long blocks of copy are boring, and when your reader sees a page that's nothing but text they may be tempted to put the paper down and move on. Give them some eye candy and they'll be more likely to hang around a bit longer.

Writing Process and Style Guidelines

There are certain types of corporate cultures that prefer content written in the traditional academic style. You don't necessarily need to be as

16 https://www.prsa.org/Intelligence/Tactics/Articles/view/10893/1103/30_3_30_Redux_How_Can_You_Reach_Today_s_Online_Rea#.V9VngJMrL-Y

formal in your white paper structure, but if you're in an industry that prefers formal or industry language, such as science, law, technology or medicine, you're better off sticking to the formula.

Before you get started putting pen to paper, have it clear in your mind the person who will get the most from the information you share in your white paper. Your most important consideration is the reader. You wouldn't play death metal rock music for a person who writes fan letters to Yanni, and you wouldn't serve hot chili peppers to a person with bleeding ulcers.

How will your white paper be filtered? In other words, what is your reader's motivation for reading it? If it's a journalist, for example, she's on deadline and she's really glad you've sent her information that's relevant to her audience. Industry analysts like information relevant to their audiences, too, and how your topic fits into the industry landscape. Engineers, business owners and key decision makers are interested in learning more about your solution and need to be assured that it actually works and is an improvement on what they're doing now.

It's not absolutely critical to understand or consider where your reader is in the sales cycle. If you understand your target audience well, then that question answers itself. Focus more on offering thought leadership. Educate your reader on what's possible. Propose money-saving alternatives. Explain how the sausage is made. Let them know what's coming down the pike.

The more people who read your white paper, the better your chance of closing the deal.

Once you are certain that you really understand the person who will be reading your white paper and are certain you are giving them the information they need and will appreciate, it's time to think of a great title.

Here's an exercise that we do in the live PR Breakthrough™ Publicity workshops that I think will help you. This gives you an opportunity to get really specific about what you do, break down what you do into little tiny pieces. A lot of people take for granted what they do or what they know.

For example, say your profession is public relations, and that you've been in the field for 30 years. As you're thinking though your white paper, you mustn't assume that everyone else in the world knows everything about public relations. Because you've been living in the world of public relations for decades, it's easy for you to assume that everyone else knows what you know. They don't. The things that seem so obvious and self-evident to you about public relations are things very few non-PR professionals know. They don't even know that they don't know it.

With a white paper, here's your opportunity to step up and share what you know with thousands and thousands of people who need to know about, and benefit from, the precious knowledge you have locked up inside your brilliant brain.

Are you a plumber or plumbing company? Suppose your reader is a recently divorced woman who knows nothing whatsoever about home maintenance, and about plumbing in particular. Her ex-husband used to do all of that stuff. Get a piece of paper and list up to 10 things she needs to know so that she can function competently. How does she fix a dripping faucet? How would she deal with a backed up toilet? How would she prevent her pipes from freezing?

Reading your white paper will give her great comfort and reassurance, and she knows that should any of these problems arise, you're the one who knows how to fix them. She's much more likely to call you for help than she is to fix the problem herself.

Your white paper doesn't have to be a list of tips; however, this kind of content is very popular with readers. Other approaches for white papers that are popular are "how-to" pieces, or in-depth explorations of the origins of something, or answering the question "Why?"

With your specific audience in mind, it's time to do some ***research.*** There are two main types of research in academic papers: primary and secondary. Research shows your reader that your conclusions are valid and objective.

Primary research is about conducting your own investigations and talking to people. It's information you discover or uncover on your own by surveys, interviews and observation. I recommend you always be doing some kind of primary research. Your findings are "newsworthy" and some may be worth pitching to the media. The more people you interview or survey, the better. Your findings may not necessarily be scientifically or statistically valid, but still, your conclusions are enough to put together an interesting white paper.

Secondary research is information you find from existing sources, i.e., books and magazine articles. Whatever the topic you're writing about in your white paper, it's highly likely someone else has explored the topic in depth. Look for statistics, quotes and factoids. Make charts and tables to illustrate your findings.

Keep track of the source of your information, and be sure to credit the originator in your white paper via footnotes or bibliography. Cite your sources! I'll say it again. Cite your sources! It's vital for credibility. Don't plagiarize. Plagiarism is *bad*. If plagiarism is something that gets you kicked out of college, it'll get you kicked out of the media, too.

The Ingredients

Not all white papers look alike or have the exact same elements, but remember what we said earlier about knowing what the rules are so that you can break them? White papers ought to include the following elements in order to preserve the integrity of the document, but you're free to label your sections differently. The purists among us, however, are expecting to see all of the following information in your white paper:

* **Executive Summary**. This is a brief, concise recap of the white paper in a few paragraphs. It's for someone who's not necessarily going to read the whole thing. Think "Cliffs Notes." Write this last.
* **The Problem**. This shows your audience that you understand and appreciate their situation. Answer the following questions: *What is the problem that needs to be solved? Who is affected by this problem? What if a solution isn't found? What then?*

* **The History**: This part of the paper helps you further gain the trust of your reader. It demonstrates that you truly understand the problem. Some readers especially enjoy taking a stroll down memory lane. Describe the milestones, events and developments that have taken us to the present day. How did things used to get done? How long has the problem existed?
* **The Solution:** This is usually the longest section of a white paper. It's here that you present your vision of the best solution(s), but be careful! Don't sell! Refer to the solution in a general way, but if you start talking about the specifics of a product, the readers will smell a sales pitch and stop reading. Answer these questions: *How does the solution you present affect the reader? How does it solve the problem?*
* **The Benefits**: Many white paper writers include the benefits within the solution section. However, this is an excellent place to insert a real-life example, or case study, of how your solution produced great results/transformation for a person or company. This section should answer the following questions: *What will the reader get if he does what you suggest? What benefits will occur, and to what degree? Where should he go to look for help? How does he find a vendor?*
* **The Conclusion/Call to Action**: This last paragraph summarizes the problem and solution, and even presents a vision for the future. It reiterates the most important point(s) you want the reader to recall from the white paper. You want the reader to feel compelled to go and find a solution like the one the white paper describes. The call to action can be as simple as, "contact [your name] at [email address] or [phone number].
* **About Company**: Remember the "company backgrounder" you created for your press kit? Cut and paste it here.

Use outside editors. When you've reached the end of the rainbow and you've drafted your white paper and cleaned it up as much as possible, show it to skilled proofreaders. Use two kinds of proofreaders: people who are subject matter experts or fact checkers, and people who are skilled editors. A good editor will fix poorly written passages and also correct spelling and grammatical errors. Do not skip this step. Just one typo will ruin the entire project.

Ways to Promote Your White Paper

After you have written your white paper and have had it professionally edited, designed and converted into a PDF, it's time to let the world know it exists so that the right people can find it and benefit by it.

In Chapter 11, "Making Contact," you'll learn how to find the journalists and content gatekeepers who are most receptive to your subject matter. Through your research, you'll learn how they like to be contacted, and when. Some of them may want to do an entire story about the topic of your white paper, and they may want to interview you. Others may want to prepare a story about the topic in general, and you might be just one of the several people they quote in the piece. In either case, your "credibility factor" goes up a notch in the eyes of readers and journalists.

What media outlet do you want to impress the most? Which one of them will put a feather in your cap when they talk about your white paper or interview you? Those are the folks to whom you direct your **pitch letter.** Also, you can send a **press release** to all of the pertinent media outlets announcing that you've written a white paper on such-and-such a topic.

If you're interested in building your mailing list, offer your white paper as a "free download" from the home page of your website or from a special lead page.

Use all of the many channels available to you to talk about your white paper and repurpose the content again and again.

Case Studies

A case study is the story of how you served a particular client and how they benefitted from your solution. It's usually two pages in length, is attractively designed and includes illustrations or images. You can offer your case studies in the press kit, on a "case study" section on your website, take them with you to trade shows as handouts, use as blog posts or newsletter articles and put them in your sales packets. They also make great videos.

Case studies, typically, are broken into three main sections: situation, challenge, and solution. The ***situation*** is a paragraph or two about the customer, using the five Ws: who, what, when, where, why. The ***challenge*** is a brief description of the "pain" the customer was experiencing before you came along. The ***solution*** explains how your product or service addressed the challenge and the results that were achieved.

The case study is a wonderful way to demonstrate your competence to people who have just recently stumbled into your presence. It also helps people understand exactly what it is you do by seeing your solution in practical application.

A Word About Being of Service

A business, or corporation, is an entity engaged in providing a product or service that fulfills a consumer or market need. But it's not always the product or service that drives your communications with the outside world. It's *you*. No matter what the organization, what drives it are its people.

One of my mentors, internationally best selling author Colin Tipping[17], says that a business can be likened to a living organism, comprised of the energy of its people. Furthering this metaphor, the membrane around an organism is permeable, meaning substances can be excreted, while simultaneously, light, air and nutrition can be absorbed. So it is with communication.

You'll hear the thought leaders say things like, "I'm not in the banking business, I'm in the customer service business." What business are you *really* in? Are you in the insurance business, or are you in the family

17 http://colintipping.com/

protection business? Are you in the estate planning business, or are you in the freedom from worry business? Whoever *you* are, whatever your deepest dreams and desires are about life and being of service, is the business you're really in.

I know an older gentleman who's been a wealth manager for years, and who has a very strong and loyal client base. On weekends, he and his wife drive to the Chesapeake Bay and take their beautiful sailboat out for a spin. When he gets back to the office, he writes about it, how the water's surface was like glass, how the wind blew through his beloved wife's hair, and some of the thoughts he had about life as he adjusted the sails. He doesn't say a word about retirement planning. This man is in the "living your dreams" business. He knows his audience well and communicates accordingly. They're affluent baby boomers with an appreciation for the finer pursuits: sailing, wine, a stroll through a Tuscany hillside village.

Who is your ideal customer? How did your reptilian brain just answer this question? It shouted, "I want customers!" Right? Well, who are your customers? Where are they in their lives? Do they have children? Are they children? What do you, personally, have in common with them that you can share as a middle ground? Find this out, communicate it through all of your different communications channels, and invite a dialog.

Repurpose

"Waste not, want not," the saying goes. Many of the pieces of content you write or produce are eligible for recycling or for turning into different iterations. A white paper, for example, can be sliced into a series of several blogs. Sections of it can also be re-enacted on video. Words and pictures always go together, like peanut butter and jelly or pork chops and applesauce.

A friend of mine applied herself to writing one blog a week for a year. That's 52 blogs. She was careful to keep them evergreen, meaning in all but a few instances the content could live forever without fear of being dated. Some will need a refresh, but still, her labor is minimal. The next year, she ran the same blogs again and reached new audiences. After all, audiences churn and refresh.

My podcast, "Media Pro Spotlight," is another example of how content can be presented in different forms. With every episode, I produce a transcript, averaging at about 10 pages. When I've produced 15 or so episodes, I publish the collection of transcripts as an eBook and promote it as a free download so that I can build my audience, and also serve them by providing a different sort of access to valuable information.

Videos go to audio recordings, which go to transcripts, which go to blog posts, which go to eBooks, which become lead magnets, which grow your audience. A good piece of content, in whatever form, has the potential to create a flowing stream of information to your audiences. Your only limit is your imagination.

Take the Chapter 9 Quiz

Score 100 percent on every chapter quiz for your chance to win free tuition for the PR Breakthrough™ Publicity Boot Camp:

http://bit.ly/2gmqdHo

Chapter 10

How to Get Story Ideas

"What you say in silence in front of no one, say it loud in front of the crowds!"

— MEHMET MURAT ILDAN

Ideas for stories, pitches, blogs, videos, white papers, newsletters, articles—content—are all around you if you open your mind and know where to look. This chapter is meant to give you a little inspiration. Use it as a reference whenever you feel stuck.

Even journalists and professional writers attend workshops when they want to restock their mental cupboards with tips and tricks for thinking up story ideas. Sometimes we get so bogged down by monkey chatter that we forget to see what's been in front of us all along.

To illustrate this point, my daughter, Jessie, (who is wise beyond her 28 years), pulled me out of a funk by reminding me that, at times, we're blind to the universe of options that surround us on a daily basis. Our best insights at times are those when we suddenly see something that's been there all along, things we couldn't see before because we were too caught up by the foggy peril of our own, self-limiting thinking.

"C'mon," said Jessie. "I'll prove it to you." I got behind the wheel of my car, and she slid into the passenger seat. "Let's find purple!" she said. We drove about 100 yards, and my daughter said, "Purple!" I looked to where she pointed, to a bush laden with purple blooms. For the next couple of hours, Jessie spotted purple cars, purple billboards, purple lights, purple buildings and purple dog leashes. It made me happy, her seeing these things. But I saw nothing, and I tried really, really hard.

That was three days ago. I'd forgotten about our search for purple. But this morning, before I sat down to write these words, I gazed out through the screened patio windows and saw purple. Lots of it—a purple flower, a purple bush, the neighbor's purple lawnmower, a purple car parked on the street, and a woman wearing purple yoga pants raising the purple flag on her mailbox. That evening, as I sipped wine with friends, I noticed the label on the wine bottle. It said, "Purple." The "purple" message had sunk in and had demonstrated itself to me like a burst of fireworks for my viewing pleasure.

Such it is with creativity and inspiration. It comes to us unexpected, with little or no effort, when our minds are calm, open and relaxed. Until Jessie had said, "Let's find purple," I'd not had purple on my mind. So for you, let me be Jessie and declare, "Let's find story ideas!" In time, they will flow to you with ease. Following are numerous ways to find story ideas or stimulate your thinking:

* **Editorial Calendars.** Most media outlets have some kind of planning schedule that organizes the material they'll cover over a period of time. Magazines, in particular, plan out their issues a year in advance, and they publish an editorial calendar. The calendar will tell you that in April, for example, they'll be focusing on Easter egg hunts, single motherhood, great chefs and scrapple recipes. It will tell you when the deadline is, too. You can access editorial calendars by visiting the magazine's website. If you don't see an obvious link to it, look for it in their "media kit."

The media kit is a resource for advertisers. If you manufacture scrapple, for example, it might be worth your while to purchase an ad in the April issue. If you are a chef, you may want to pitch the magazine so that they'll include you in the editorial coverage about chefs in April. Don't see it on the website or in the media kit? Call and ask them to send it to you. NOTE: Magazine issues are planned out many months in advance. During the summer, they're thinking about Christmas. When you're shoveling show from your driveway, they're thinking of the 4th of July.

* **Holiday Calendars.** Type "holiday calendar" into your Internet browser and you'll pull up all kinds of fun facts. The holiday calendar is immensely helpful to you as you plan out your annual publicity campaigns and content strategy. You'll also find on the internet lists of special events, some of them truly wacky,[18] that were invented to support various retail agendas (e.g., greeting card companies and flower delivery sites) but you can still leverage them to your advantage. There's National Grandparents Day, Bring Your Daughter to Work Day, and Make Your Dreams Come True Day. What can you arrange to do in your business that ties into a holiday or event?
* **Employee or Team-Related News.** Local newspapers and business publications commonly have sections where they print announcements about new hires and promotions. Check in with your employees regularly to take inventory on their hobbies or outside interests, or any awards or recognitions they won in the community. Your organization is comprised of people, and the more well thought of your people are, the more esteemed your brand becomes in the marketplace. When possible, engage your employees to participate as a team to support community or non-profit events, e.g., 5K races, park cleanups, building projects and food drives. These make great human-interest stories.

---

18 http://www.timeanddate.com/holidays/fun/

Sometimes we get so bogged down by monkey chatter that we forget to see what's been in front of us all along.

* **Company Milestones.** If you're celebrating a significant anniversary, try to think of interesting experiences or insights you've had since being in business. What led you to go into business in the first place? Have you changed your focus since then? Why? If you're an entrepreneur who's enjoyed success, what advice can you share with the rest of us poor, struggling souls? How can you help others to succeed based upon your experience?
* **Industry Trends.** Keep in mind that journalists in your industry are hungry for content. More important, they are short-staffed and can't stay on top of new developments in the industry without our help. Keep your antennae up for industry news: management shake-ups, mergers and acquisitions, legislation that has an impact, new paradigms, new inventions, new thought leaders. If you can step up and provide comment on any of these trends, send a pitch letter. If you're not able to comment but recognize the trend as significant, write your media contacts a note that says something to the effect of, "Here's a new development in the industry that I thought you might be interested in."
* **Surveys, Opinion Polls and Primary Research.** The media loves to run stories having to do with research, statistics and public opinion. Pepsi ran a famous campaign many years ago called the "Pepsi Challenge." They set up tables in public places and invited people to taste two beverages (Coke and Pepsi) and say which one they preferred. The results of this blind taste test revealed that most Americans preferred the taste of Pepsi. Though the campaign was criticized for being scientifically invalid, the "public opinion" news value of it received national attention for years.

  With tools like Survey Monkey and Google Forms readily available for free, it's easy to conduct surveys and opinion polls of selected audiences. Your goal is to get as many responses as possible from as many people as possible. When you've tabulated the results, explain your findings in a report and tell the media about it. There are other ways to use the research, too. For instance, you can offer your research report as a "free download" to the audience you think will be most interested.

* **Current Events.** Remember the concept of "newsjacking," i.e., offering your expertise in reaction to timely issues or breaking news stories? Good public relations professionals read, watch and listen to everything they can get their hands on, primarily with this principle in mind. Set aside as much as an hour every day to catch up on what's going on in your community, state, country and in the world. Doing so also stimulates ideas for speaking topics, blogs and newsletter articles. It's your duty to serve the world with the knowledge or skills with which you've been gifted. If what you know or do provides clarity or solves problems, then staying in touch with what's going on in the world enables you to serve on a much wider scale than if you seal yourself up behind closed company doors.
* **Customer Stories.** This is more of a public relations move than a publicity tactic, but as you probably have learned by now, customers say the darndest things. By listening to their conversation and feedback, you'll get all kinds of ideas for videos, opinion polls and new products. Visit with your customers and find out what's going on in their lives and businesses. In many instances, you'll hear a story that's newsworthy, and in that case, offer to share it with your media contacts. It's a goodwill gesture all around. Your customer is grateful for the publicity, and your media contact is grateful for the tip. Whether your contact uses the story is less important than you having shared potentially useful information.

You might also keep your customers in mind when a major news story breaks and you know of a customer or two who's a subject matter expert who your media contacts might be interested in interviewing (with the customer's blessing, of course). Again, it's a win-win situation.

* **Strategic Alliances.** Sometimes, a story idea is bigger than what we can offer on our own. Consider partnering with entities in your industry to create newsworthy events. Having this greater input lends credibility to your pitch, but also, you're saving journalists hours of tracking down sources to interview and images to capture.

  I've had great luck with getting big stories by working strategically with other organizations. A simple example of this is when I organized a groundbreaking ceremony for a bank's new LEED-certified brick-and-mortar branch in Philadelphia. We invited the mayor, and his public relations team worked with us to attract several important media outlets to the event. It's great working with **members of local government** to co-create publicity opportunities. The more highly ranked the politician, the more likely he/she has a press secretary or team of public relations interns with whom you can combine power and influence.

The media loves to run stories having to do with research results.

  Strategic alliances with customers work well, too. One of my client's customers was a Greyhound rescue organization that was raising funds to build an addition to its facility. We helped them get media attention by pitching stories about greyhounds, e.g., how they're mistreated, the true nature of the breed, and touching rescue success stories. The campaign ran for several months, garnered a ton of media coverage (compelling dog stories are almost guaranteed to attract interest) and the organization exceeded its fundraising goals. Moreover, the customer had plenty of nice things to say about my client, and they referred business often to my client.

* **Create a Special Event**. Back in the 1990s, I worked with a computer aided design (CAD) firm that was a value-added reseller

for Autodesk and Bentley Systems, two of the largest CAD software systems in the market at the time. We put together our own trade show and called it "CADfest," attracted exhibitors who targeted, as we did, AEC firms[19], sent out massive invitations, and of course, created a press kit and solicited media coverage. The event did incredibly well on all fronts and everyone benefited.

Another client of mine was the merchant association at a posh, local shopping center that was languishing from lack of customer traffic. My team created a full-day event to attract affluent mommies and their kids. Several local dignitaries, including the mayor, kicked in with resources and we attracted more than 1,000 visitors. The event also garnered stories in both print and broadcast media, yielding more than a million impressions. On the heels of this success, the shopping center continued to create special events to attract repeat traffic from affluent shoppers.

Special events are wonderful because of the strategic alliances that are built, the opportunity to grow your mailing list, and for building brand awareness.

* **Contests.** Contests are effective for their human-interest story value. I helped my client, a local community bank, run many contests throughout the year because the bank sought to increase foot traffic in its brick and mortar branches. (This is the problem for many brick-and-mortar businesses. Shoppers are going online.) We ran pumpkin-decorating contests during Halloween, 4th of July coloring contests and back-to-school essay contests. When winners of the contests were chosen, we publicized the results, which were almost always picked up by the local newspapers, and further established the bank's brand as a contributing member of the community.
* **Brainstorm**. If you hit a drought and can't think of story ideas to save your life, then bring together a bunch of people you like

19 Architectural, engineering, construction

and trust, buy them a pizza, ply them with alcohol, and make the theme of your party, "20 Ways I'm Newsworthy." Let them get as wild and silly as they want, because you're going to get ideas you never would have thought of on your own. For example, an attorney friend of mine volunteered to chair the fundraising committee of his favorite charity, and he needed ideas of how to promote their annual campaign. Someone suggested that the charity's executive director agree to shave his head if they reached their fundraising goal. It's not a new idea; charities and nonprofits pull stunts like this all the time, to the delight of their donors. The point is, my friend would never have thought of such an outlandish idea on his own. The fundraising campaign was a success, the guy shaved his head, and the media came in droves to shoot pictures and video.

* **Keyword Searches.** This is a method for generating a list of story ideas that's often overlooked. All I can say is, "Yay, Google!" Type in some industry keywords and see what comes up. I just typed, "architectural innovation," into the search window and was given 963,000 results in 0.62 seconds, with trends and studies galore. There's nothing new under the sun, so feel free to piggyback on the work and ideas of others, giving it your own, original fingerprint. As you churn out content based upon the material you found in your search, remember to cite your sources.
* **H.A.R.O.** This is a free site that journalists use to post stories they're working on and asking for responses from subject matter experts. The initials stand for, "Help A Reporter Out."[20] When you sign up, H.A.R.O. will send you daily emails with lists of stories that journalists need help with. If you see a story request about your industry or within your realm of expertise, your next step is to write a well-crafted pitch letter that clearly explains why

20 https://www.helpareporter.com/

you're the best person to interview for the story. Try it! If nothing else, it's great pitch writing practice.

* **Your Life.** I don't buy insurance from a person because he/she did such a great job of reminding me that I was going to die some day or that home burglary is a constant threat. I bought insurance from a person with whom I could relate as a person. In fact, I bought insurance from a guy (I'll call him "Mike") who is a musician, like me, and who loves music, as I do. Mike's blog and LinkedIn posts are not about long-term disability insurance, but about fine musical instruments, the concerts he's gone to, other people who have day jobs but who are also musicians, or profiles of musicians he's admired over the years. His communication with customers and prospects is easy because he talks about a subject he loves. Mike lets his website and LinkedIn profile explain what he does for a living, but his personal area of interest starts the conversation and provides frequent and welcome opportunities for engagement.

What do the media and newsworthy story ideas have to do with this? Remember that "the media" is one of your most important target audiences. What does the media want from you? Newsworthy stories. They have space to fill, and you can help. Thus, Mike has built a list of media contacts who are interested in stories about music. (I'll explain how to go about building relationships with journalists in the next chapter.) He's been very useful to his music journalist friends by providing the occasional tip. He also writes a column about the local music scene for a community newspaper. He gets a byline, and also a short blurb about his insurance business at the end of the article. Mike is considering putting together a local music festival with some business colleagues who are also musicians: a trust attorney, a wealth manager and a guy who owns a local recording studio. This uses the strategies of "strategic alliances" and "special events" we discussed previously.

Take the Chapter 10 Quiz

Score 100 percent on every chapter quiz for your chance to win free tuition for the PR Breakthrough™ Publicity Boot Camp:

http://bit.ly/2gC77Q8

Chapter 11

Making Contact

"You can't stay in your corner of the forest
waiting for others to come to you.
You have to go to them sometimes."

— *A. A. Milne, Winnie the Pooh*

Hopefully by now you have a better understanding of one of your most challenging but beneficial audiences: journalists and media professionals. We must respect this group as the treasured few who have the power to make us, or break us. Our goal is to earn our way into their inner circle, because once inside we enjoy certain privileges that are known to few others.

It's not so different to build relationships with journalists as it is to build relationships with any other important segment. It all starts with research to understand their points of view, behavior, motivations and how they prefer to consume information. Next, it's our mission to establish credibility, gain trust and give generously, without overt ulterior motives. And last, we maintain a continuous, reliable presence that shows unwavering respect for our audience's needs and a sincere desire to accommodate those needs.

We must strive to create relationships that are mutually beneficial. We're all in business, after all, with professional obligations to fulfill. It's understood. Journalists understand completely that when we make a pitch or send a press release that our agenda is to benefit from the publicity. We're all grown-ups here. It's okay to be up front. The media craves good content, and we supply it—the ultimate barter.

So, let's dig in.

By the way, in this chapter, I haven't included the social media channels, because they're not germane to this particular conversation. Rather, this chapter will stick with the traditional media outlets, i.e., newspapers, magazines, wire services, television and radio. I also threw blogs in here, because many are written by journalists and require your help with the delivery of content.

Types of Media Outlets

Newspapers. The newspaper is the oldest and most established type of media outlet, and may be one of the first to perish in this age of digital communication. The debate rages on about whether the newspaper will become obsolete in our lifetimes.

If this paper-based medium is destined to perish, then it's certainly dying a slow death. Publishers continue to fight to remain relevant and reinvent their models, but in the meantime, staffs are decreasing and advertising revenue has shrunk. There is still an audience that enjoys the feel of paper in their hands. Personally, one of my favorite Sunday morning rituals is to sit in a comfy chair, a cup of coffee and a plate of Entenmann's crumb cake at my side, consuming sections of a major metropolitan newspaper, like the *New York Times.*

Just as there are many different kinds of media outlets, there are many different kinds of newspapers: the big dailies with circulations into the hundreds of thousands, the weeklies, the monthlies, the community newspapers, newspapers targeted to certain ethnic or religious populations, and also tabloids that focus on particular segments of the local market such as fitness, parenting, liberal and entertainment publications.

Most newspapers have similar editorial structures, i.e., an editor who is responsible for determining which content will appear in each issue and who assigns the writing to his staff of reporters and freelancers.

Magazines. Magazines are print-based publications with specific niches in any area of interest you can imagine—beauty, sports, celebrity gossip, parenting, semiconductor manufacturing, dogs, wine—whatever your expertise, there's a four-color glossy magazine, perhaps several of them, ready to serve its audience and advertisers.

This is another medium people prefer to read in paper form, leafing through the pages, reading articles and cutting out pictures for their vision boards. Your doctor's office, coffee shop, airplane or hair salon is a popular magazine reading venue. (Hopefully, your doctor isn't a bass fishing aficionado or golf digest subscriber, or else your choice of magazines will be limited and, disappointed, you'll go back to playing Candy Crush on your iPhone. Or maybe that's just me.)

What's your industry or area of subject matter expertise? For fun, type your specialty into your search engine address field and add the word "magazine" to the end. It's likely you'll be given hundreds of choices.

Magazines have longer shelf lives than newspapers. The magazines in waiting rooms are often left sitting in the rack for months, so there's a strong chance that each issue is read dozens of times. A magazine's "pass along rate" is important to advertisers, and it's a boon to you if you've managed to place an article in there.

Magazines plan their issues months in advance, so they're not typically concerned with breaking news. Rather, a magazine's stories tend to explore topical issues in greater detail, and articles can be as long as 5,000 words or more, depending upon the target audience.

Most magazines produce editorial calendars that you can download from their websites. The editorial calendar tells us what kind of content or coverage is planned for each issue over the next year. Their websites will also tell you when their deadlines are and also give you a list of the editors and writers they keep on staff.

It's not so different to build relationships with journalists as it is to build relationships with any other important segment. It all starts with research to understand their points of view, behavior, motivations and how they prefer to receive information.

Wire Services. *I say tomato, you say tomahto.*[21] You say news agency, I say wire service. They're both the same thing.

Wire services became popular after the invention of the telegraph, and it was a great thing for newspapers that could now print news and top stories from around the world. Examples of news services to which media outlets subscribe include the Associated Press, Reuters and PR Newswire. There are also business, science and health newswires.

If you have a breaking news story or something that's extremely newsworthy that you think people outside of your local region will appreciate, it's appropriate to send a well-written press release to a wire service.

Television. Television has the potential to reach millions of people. The networks reach audiences both locally and across the country, and of course, hundreds of cable stations have popped up that allow for greater segmentation and geographic targeting than ever before.

The Holy Grail for the author of a book or someone who wants to be a leading expert in his or her field is an appearance on a nationally syndicated news or talk show. I've seen authors and speakers go from paupers to princesses overnight because of an appearance on Oprah or some other top tier television program.

Modern technology has made it possible for you to be on national television from a small room in your hometown. We use satellites and green screens to make it look like you're broadcasting live from the nation's capital, when you're really in an office or at home. We call these "SMT" interviews, or satellite media tours.

---

21 "Let's Call the Whole Thing Off," written by George and Ira Gershwin for the 1937 film, "Shall We Dance," starring Fred Astaire and Ginger Rogers. https://youtu.be/zZ3fjQa5Hls

Television is a visual medium. Pictures and video footage are everything, so when you're pitching for television you need to explain the entire "package" for editors and producers. You can offer to shoot pictures and video yourself, or you can tell them about the kinds of opportunities for photos and images that would be available to their news team. Cover the logistics details and set up the interviews. Be specific in what kinds of images are possible so that the editor or producer can see the story in his/her head. If you don't have a fully formed story in mind, the overworked TV producer will probably pass in favor of stories that are better developed and ready to go.

If your mission is to be interviewed on camera, talking about your new book or demonstrating how to make the world's best potato salad, consider getting some media training. We will sharpen your interview skills in Chapter 14.

A few more words about getting on big network TV talk shows and news programs: There are so-called PR experts out there who will tell you they can get you on Oprah or Good Morning America within a few weeks. Unless you're already a celebrity or public figure, this is absolutely untrue. It's like telling people they'll win the lottery just by buying one ticket. To make promises like this is pandering to people's lust for quick riches and overnight fame (without having to do the hard work).

Even if you're a superstar in the making, an absolute genius (evidenced by your purchase of this book), it can take months, or even years of persistence, hard work and a well-honed, beautifully articulated expertise to earn a spot on national television. There is no such thing as an overnight sensation. As a business coach friend of mine likes to say, "You don't go to bed a blunder and wake up a wonder."

I want you to succeed. I want you to get these big gigs. But let's work together first to groom your ability to deliver great story ideas on a consistent basis. Slow and steady wins the race, and if you're realistic and don't give up, you'll get there, and more importantly, stay there.

Radio. According to the FCC, there are 15,406[22] licensed radio stations in the United States. Chances are good that with a good topic and the ability to speak articulately about it, you can land many radio talk show interviews.

Nonprofit organizations use Public Service Announcements (PSAs) to get the word out via radio. I have included a sample of a PSA in the "Samples & Resources" section at the end of this book. You may submit these to the station via an MP3, or they might read it live. Stations don't do as many PSAs as they used to, and even then, these types of free announcements would be made in the wee hours when the world was asleep—not really impactful. Aim more, rather, for guest interviews on public service programs.

Podcasts. I mention podcasts because they are quickly gaining popularity by people who enjoy listening to targeted content on their mobile devices. Although radio still commands the lion's share of audio listeners,[23] podcast content offers you an additional opportunity to gain exposure for your topic, since podcasts, like magazines, are tightly segmented and many feature interviews with subject matter experts.

Blogs. There are, reportedly, 152 million blogs on the Internet.[24] This number includes all of the companies who publish blogs on their websites. There are also blogs that are produced by professional writers whose readerships count in the millions.

Similar to the other media outlets we've talked about, blogs come in all shapes and sizes. To a large extent, the big blogs rely heavily on guest-contributed content, so be sure to research the blogosphere and add any relevant blogs to your list of media outlets.

---

22 http://www.radioworld.com/article/how-many-radio-stations-are-there-in-the-united-states/269915

23 http://www.journalism.org/2016/06/15/podcasting-fact-sheet/

24 http://www.wpvirtuoso.com/how-many-blogs-are-on-the-internet/

How to Make a Media List

There are many different ways to make a media list, but before you begin, the first step is to ask members of your target audience and customers what they read, watch or listen to. Also, ask anyone else who has a vested interest in you or your business. For example, if you're a startup company with a board of advisors who are well grounded in your industry, ask them what outlets they consult to stay current on what's going on in the world. What are your favorite sources for keeping current? Trade magazines? The local metropolitan daily newspaper? Early morning TV news? Write all of these sources down.

I use Excel spreadsheets to collect all of my media contact information, but it doesn't matter how you collect and store your media contact info, just as long as the system you use allows you to easily keep track of your activity and make updates when you need to. The fields on my spreadsheet are first name, last name, job title, media outlet name, email address, mailing address, phone number, a brief description of the media outlet, deadline and editorial opportunities (e.g., upcoming issues covering your topic). I also have a "remarks" section that allows me to record notes and conversations.

Start your media list by researching local media outlets, and then work your way outward. Local outlets are the low-hanging fruit in your media relations orchard because of the rules of "proximity" and "relevance."

If your time and resources are limited, be kind to yourself. You don't need an exhaustive media list all at once. Build it a couple of outlets or journalists at a time. Your media list will always be a work in progress, and it will grow and become more comprehensive over time. If you're lucky, you might run into a non-competing colleague who already has a media list of journalists who are interested in your subject matter. Though some people are protective of their media lists and hide them like cold war spies hide microfilm, there are also strategic partners with an abundance consciousness who will share. (My PR Breakthrough™ Client Forum on Facebook, which is a closed group comprised of people who have attended my workshops, is a place where such sharing takes place.)

The Holy Grail for the author of a book or someone who wants to be a leading expert in his or her field is an appearance on a nationally syndicated news or talk show.

You can purchase local and national media lists, and find free resources online. A simple Google search on "[city name] media list" will pull up all of the many resources available to you at little or no cost. The reference section at the library has directories that provide information on the nation's media outlets. Go to your favorite newsstand and pick up copies of all the publications you think might be a fit for your industry or expertise. Similarly, flip on your TV or radio and make note of the stations and channels that attract your target audience.

Every now and then, I create a media list for a metropolitan area somewhere in the U.S. and offer it as a free download. If you'd like one, send me a note via email (dana@danadobson.com) telling me what city you're in and I'll send you the link.

If you can afford it, and are a large regional or national business with multiple product lines, and if you are going to establish an in-house public relations department and staff it with people whose sole responsibility is to pitch stories and market content, then you have the option of subscribing to an online media database. We use Cision, which has swallowed up major competitors like Vocus and PR Newswire. Cision gives me up to date information on any media contact or outlet I need: names, addresses, preferred methods of contact, deadlines and more. It's not always completely accurate (because media people move around a lot) but it gives me a good head start. For us, it's a useful tool because we have several clients and it saves us hours of research time.

Download the editorial calendars from all of the magazines on your list. Many of these are easily accessible online, but if you don't see it, it's okay to call and ask. They're happy to oblige, just in case you're a potential advertiser. If you see an issue on the editorial calendar that's going to focus on your industry or area of expertise, call or email the editor to confirm it.

Sometimes magazines, especially local/regional lifestyle magazines, do not release their editorial calendars because they don't want their competitors to know what they're up to. Their public editorial calendar is published to attract certain advertisers at certain times of the year, but the editorial calendar will be top secret. That's why you need to call to confirm.

Now that you have some names on your list, it's time to begin the relationship building process, and you'll do this the same way you'd build any other relationship. Based on the hundreds of conversations I've had with editors, producers and reporters over the years, I stick to a process that has served me well.

First, before reaching out, I spend time finding out as much about my contact as possible online. I read their articles, watch their shows or YouTube videos and look at their social media profiles. If they're columnists or talk show hosts, I make note of their tone and style.

My next step is to send a nice letter of introduction via email. I let them know that I've familiarized myself with their previous work and compliment them on any pieces that I thought were especially good. Because I'm a publicist who represents clients, I'll let them know that I have a client who's an expert on [topic that matches the contact's beat or focus]. I explain that it's my goal to be a resource for them, and that I look forward to establishing a good relationship by sharing useful information and assisting them when they need access to industry inside information or quotable experts. If they work for a local media outlet, I invite them for coffee or a meal.

After that, as much as is humanly possible, I monitor their online and professional activity. If something interesting is going on in the world that's pertinent to what they cover, I'll send them a quick note and offer to help if they need it.

I promise you, if you do your research, follow the rules of etiquette and communicate with respect with the people on your media list, you will become a trusted resource, and maybe even a friend. Not overnight, perhaps—you'll have to prove yourself. Your emails might be arbitrarily deleted at the beginning because they don't yet know that you are a great person—but your having done your homework is going to make you very successful in media relations.

There have been times when it's taken me months to establish a rapport with a reporter. Be professional, and persist. Remember, they're inundated with emails from unprofessional people they don't know on a daily basis. Anyone would become suspicious and cynical after regular waves of assault. It takes time to earn respect and trust.

It's the quality of your pitches that will make the difference. You can get your foot in the door very quickly if you consistently deliver newsworthy story ideas, even if you and the assignment editor aren't yet acquainted.

Keep your list up to date. Sometimes it seems that just when you've developed a good relationship with a journalist, they move on. If an email is returned, find out immediately who the new contact is, and start the process from scratch. Hopefully the contact who left has moved to a different outlet in the same industry, so you'll still have that relationship.

I'm often asked by potential clients, "Do you have contacts in the [blank] industry?" It's the wrong question to ask. It's a good story that earns a journalist's attention, not the fact that the two of you are buddies. If you are professional in your dealings with journalists and know how to pitch a story, it's irrelevant whether you and that journalist do "Tuesday Night Trivia" together at the local pub. You *still* won't get coverage if it's a bad story, or it doesn't fit the segment's requirements, or if there's breaking news that pre-empts your story.

Press Tours

The best way to establish a relationship is by meeting your important media contacts face to face. Most of the journalists in your local area are open to meeting you for coffee or for a meal. Those who are especially time crunched may invite you to come to their office for a chat.

One-on-one meetings make future pitching so much easier, because your visit has helped establish your credibility and create goodwill. It removes the pain of having to repeatedly introduce yourself and your company via repeated electronic outreach.

As a public relations professional, I make it my business to meet regularly with journalists. It's great to be able to put faces with names and to have conversations that remove barriers and establish trust. I go to these meetings as myself, not as someone who is representing a particular client. When I'm representing clients, I set up the meetings and perhaps attend to make initial introductions, but I then fade into the background while my client and the journalist build rapport.

It doesn't happen so often anymore because of the expense, but I used to take the CEOs and/or key spokespersons of companies on national press tours to meet one-on-one with their tier one media contacts. Tier one contacts are the journalists who work for the high circulation metropolitan dailies, most influential industry publications and broadcast media outlets. Sometimes these tours were purely "meet and greet." The purpose was to showcase my CEO's or spokesperson's media savvy and subject matter expertise in person.

Press tours are especially valuable for product and book launches, because your media contacts are able to see a real-time presentation of what you offer, perhaps hold your product and book in their hands, on their own turf.

Schedule press tour appointments via email with phone follow up two weeks in advance. For some reason, this time frame makes it more likely your meeting time will stick to their calendar. Good planning is the key to make sure you reach all of your appointments on time. You must think through every detail and anticipate every contingency, e.g. modes of transportation, travel time between appointments, traffic, and construction delays. Factor in weather conditions. Bring umbrellas in case it rains.

According to the FCC, there are 15,406 licensed radio stations in the United States.

I always made a binder with all of the arrangements spelled out: addresses, phone numbers, maps, itinerary and any special security or parking instructions provided by the media outlet. Also included was a profile of the media contact, photo and thorough description of their beat, previous work, style and any other relevant piece of information I could dig up. I also boxed up a large supply of press kits to use as leave behinds. Do not bring gifts—they are not ethically permitted to accept them.

The experts and spokespersons who fare the best in the world of media relations are the ones who keep the irons of these face-to-face meetings hot by staying in touch, providing relevant information and suggesting story angles that are tied to current events. It's worth your time and effort, considering the huge impact this media exposure will have on your bottom line.

Take the Chapter 11 Quiz

Score 100 percent on every chapter quiz for your chance to win free tuition for the PR Breakthrough™ Publicity Boot Camp:

http://bit.ly/2gCdXVG

Chapter 12

Personal Branding: Leveraging Your Expertise

"An image is not simply a trademark, a design,
slogan or an easily remembered picture.
It is a studiously crafted personality profile of an
individual, institution, corporation, product or service."

—*Daniel Boorstin*

"Understand your own personal DNA. Don't do things
because I do them or Steve Jobs or Mark Cuban tried it. You
need to know your personal brand and stay true to it."

— *Gary Vaynerchuk*

My mother used to tell me to always look my best, because, after all, you never knew when or where you were going to meet "Mr. Right." My mom's fondest wish for me was to marry someone financially well off and live the remainder of my life eating bonbons. It was common in that era to brainwash your daughters and equip them with the tools and talent to snag rich husbands. Ira Levin's "Stepford Wives" captures the paradigm brilliantly. I didn't realize it at the time, but my mom, one of the millions of women who drank the "June Cleaver"[25] Kool-Aid, was intent on "building my brand."

Unfortunately for her, when I turned 14 I took charge of my own brand and adopted an identity that was so in opposition to my mother's intentions that it shocks and offends her to this day. My public look, attitude and behavior were every inch the "rebellious, badass, rock star wannabe." I thought I looked fantastic. I liked my angst. She didn't.

Mom's personal brand was carefully contrived and consistent. She never left the house without her hair done, a full face of makeup, a dab of Chanel No. 5 and a flattering outfit, even if she was only going to the grocery store. She was an actress and a model, and looking good, especially in public, was tactically essential to her career success. After all, one never knows when one is going to be "discovered." When asked to describe my mom, people would have said things like, "vivacious," "beautiful," "fun" and "actress."

Has your look and style changed over the years? What is it, that *je ne sais quoi*, that you project to the world? If asked to describe you, what would people say? If you are looking to make an impact on the people around you—employees, prospects, audiences, media, community—you must cultivate a personal brand, which is an amplification of your best, authentic self, in order to inspire and motivate others.

Understanding the Importance of Personal Brand in Business

Like everything else, the notion of personal brand is nothing new. It's an idea that's been brought to the forefront with the advent of digital communications media, when developing one's public professional profile raised more frequent discussions on how one ought to present one's "business self" on LinkedIn and other channels. Our higher level of exposure

25 https://youtu.be/vnv5VGyK9zQ

to millions of new eyeballs necessitates a closer look at our personal presentation and how we are perceived by the outside world.

In her book, "Daring Greatly,"[26] Brene Brown, a researcher who studies shame and vulnerability, says that *who* you are is much more important than your business objectives. Your personal brand is how other people see you and think about you. It's what others expect of you, based upon the confident expression of your authentic self. Think of the heroes, leaders and iconic personalities who made their marks throughout history, or those you've encountered in your lifetime. Just rattling off a few who spring to mind, there's Benjamin Franklin, Abraham Lincoln, Marilyn Monroe, Groucho Marx, Andy Warhol, John Lennon, Martin Luther King, Richard Branson, Dolly Parton and most presidents of the United States. Who are the first icons who spring into your mind? What, do you think, makes them so unique and memorable?

When I was growing up in business, "brand" was a word we associated with a business entity, not a person. People did business with companies, not people. Companies developed taglines to articulate their brands in memorable ways. *Things go better with Coke. Have it your way at Burger King. Plop, plop, fizz, fizz, oh, what a relief it is. Just do it.*

As the Internet emerged and evolved, it became possible for sales people and others to network virtually on a global scale. They posted online profiles to present their best professional selves to land jobs or do business.

Leaders were skeptical of LinkedIn at first. It was a fad, they insisted. Bankers and other professionals in highly regulated industries avoided the Internet as a branding opportunity because of fear on many levels: information security, employee misuse and, most of all, change. To quote "Frankenstein" author Mary Shelly, "Nothing is so painful to the human mind as a great and sudden change."

---

26 https://www.amazon.com/Daring-Greatly-Courage-Vulnerable-Transforms/dp/1592408419/ref=sr_1_1?s=books&ie=UTF8&qid=1473596197&sr=1-1&keywords=daring+greatly

The strength of an organization's brand is as important as ever, but there is now a heightened demand to establish the personal brands of industry leaders, entrepreneurs and subject matter experts.

What's happened is that there's been a major shift in the way we perceive and promote brand. The strength of an organization's brand is as important as ever, but there is now a heightened demand to establish the personal brands of an organization's leadership, subject matter experts and customer-facing personnel. People are finally starting to get it that an organization is comprised of the energy, passion and capability of its people. Thus, it's commonplace to vet new business relationships by looking at their LinkedIn profiles, or by Googling their names. When looking for industry leaders and experts to interview, journalists go online to do their research. If you're not there, then technically, you don't exist. And if your profile is sub-par, you're off the list.

Personal Brand vs. Reputation

Having a strong personal brand is very important. It's what makes you stand out in a crowd, but your personal brand is nothing without a good reputation. Famous criminals like Al Capone and Baby Face Nelson had memorable brands, but I wouldn't want to be in the same room with either of them without a Kevlar vest and a can of mace.

Your reputation is built from the accumulation of your actions in the world. You could be the most memorable personality in the industry, but if you have a reputation for being a jerk to your employees, not keeping your word or delivering on your brand promise, then being memorable becomes a liability and a curse.

For example, if you have attempted to build a personal brand that says you care about your customers and that you and your team bends over backwards to provide the finest service, you'd better be able to deliver on that consistently. Otherwise, you suffer a damaged reputation.

Corporations have increasingly lost public trust over the years, which reflects on the personal brands of their leaders. Have you ever seen the movie, "The Corporation?"[27] It's a documentary based on the book by Joel Bakan called, "The Corporation: The Pathological Pursuit of Profit and Power." It compares some of the ways a corporation behaves to the way a psychopath behaves, such as an incapacity to maintain human relationships, the reckless disregard for the safety of others, continual lying and the inability to experience guilt or remorse.

If you are in a leadership or customer-facing position within a large organization with a questionable reputation, it's beneficial to you to establish a strong, reliable personal brand that expresses your values, passion to serve, and who you are as a human being.

Discover, Cultivate and Build Your Personal Brand

How do you think that you, as a business person, are perceived by others? There are ways to find out, if you really want to know. In my personal branding workshops, we conduct an exercise that asks participants to write down three separate impressions they get of each other after each gives a 60-second introduction of themselves. Your peers are permitted to write *positive* characteristics only, because we don't have time in the session to deal with the re-building of self-esteem. (When I work with clients as a leadership branding consultant, we do explore and ameliorate the negatives.)

To build a strong personal brand, you must have the courage to face an honest self-assessment, and also to receive frank appraisals from the people you love, trust and respect. If you really want to get down to the nitty gritty and lower your shields enough so that honest feedback can get through, then try this: Send letters, or emails, to five or six people with whom you have supportive relationships. Explain to them that you are engaged in a self-improvement exercise (assigned by a business coach)

27 https://youtu.be/KMNZXV7jOG0

that requires you to get frank opinions of yourself from people you know and trust. Ask them to give you a list of your positive characteristics, as well as any characteristics that might be holding you back from achieving your full potential in the business world. Ask them to describe the image you project to the outside world. Promise them that there will be no hard feelings, but rather deep appreciation for their courage and willingness to help you with the creation of your new personal brand.

Warning: the feedback may be emotionally difficult. Given full reign, some people may "go to town" on the list of criticisms. Breathe, and take in the feedback with grace. After all, you asked for it! Consider it market research.

I asked some close friends and colleagues I considered mentors to give me a frank appraisal of what they perceived as my strengths and weaknesses so that I could further develop my skills as a speaker and workshop leader. When I got my results back, it knocked the wind out of me. I threw up, ate a whole sleeve of Oreo cookies, and assumed the fetal position on my couch for a couple of days. Thank goodness for "I Love Lucy" and "Star Trek" reruns.

To build a strong personal brand, you must have the courage to face an honest self-assessment, and also to receive frank appraisals from the people you love, trust and respect.

It's not always easy to ask for, or receive, honest feedback, but I think you'll find that as the result of it you're able to grow into a new awareness of your unique gifts. Personal growth sometimes requires the shattering of long-held beliefs about how you are perceived by others. Some of the negatives about myself I already knew, but I thought I'd cleverly concealed them all these years. Other things were a complete shock, but they were things I could fix with practice. There were also things I could do nothing about, stuff that would require workarounds. *C'est la vie.*

If you're a leader or a subject matter expert who wants to be in the spotlight, or who is inadvertently in the spotlight and is therefore obliged to present a positive image, then you *need* to know what others think of you. Let the friendly people in your life have a whack at you before the trolls do.

The purpose of this entire exercise is to identify how you are *perceived* by others so that you can make adjustments in your professional presentation in the business world. Do not take the feedback to mean that you must change the essence of who you are. You are an amazing person with unique and powerful gifts, warts and all.

Someone wrote to me, "I get the impression that you are afraid of your audience." This is the one that made me want to eat my weight in pound cake. At the same time, though, this was incredibly useful feedback. I had no idea I was projecting this. I was completely unconscious of it. If I wanted to be an effective speaker and workshop leader, I needed to project the confidence and ease I felt inside—which meant working on my body language.[28] I was also told that I mumble. That, too, has been fixed.

Eight Characteristics of a Strong Personal Brand

This book concerns itself with positioning you or your business so that you can attract raving fans and luxuriate in the media spotlight. Perhaps you're already trained and groomed and all you need now is a set of techniques for working effectively with journalists so that you can "start spreading the news."[29]

Regardless of the stage you're in in your promotional planning, it's important to be aware of the characteristics of a strong and attractive personal brand. Think of your favorite leaders throughout history, and you'll realize that most of them exhibited the traits listed below.

The beauty of all of the following attributes is that they can be taught and learned. We've conducted workshops for organizational leaders,

---

28 There's a wonderful TED talk by Amy Cuddy about body language here: https://www.ted.com/talks/amy_cuddy_your_body_language_shapes_who_you_are?language=en

29 https://youtu.be/WcuxBf0frQE

spokespeople and subject matter experts to foster the ability to project these qualities, whether they initially claim to "feel" them or not. What's wonderful is, with the act of projecting, even pretending, comes an amazing internal shift. There are many sayings to describe this phenomenon, i.e., fake it 'til you make it, or where the body goes, the mind follows. We grow by acting "as if."

Confidence. You can tell when someone has confidence. They have an openness of gaze, eyes lifted, and seem eager to take in their surroundings. There's a special energy that comes from confidence, a readiness that's created when one's body is relaxed but alert. Confidence is being ready to have a good experience, from no matter what direction it's dealt. We project confidence with a smile, a firm handshake and eye contact.

Charisma. We used to think that charisma was an innate quality possessed by the anointed few. Some people had "it," that mysterious air that generates attention just by entering a room. Scientists now believe, however, that charisma is a trait that can be cultivated, and they have empirical evidence to prove it. You can *learn* it! According to Ronald Riggio, PhD, professor of leadership and organizational psychology at Claremont McKenna College, there are three traits that, when combined, create the phenomenon of charisma: expressiveness, control and sensitivity. [30]

My sister, Lori, has big-time charisma. I've watched her for years to try and figure out what it is about her that makes people fall in love with her so easily and completely after only a few minutes in her presence. Bill Clinton is famous for having "it," too. Lori genuinely loves people, which gives her a leg up in the whole charisma thing. But even if you're not naturally comfortable with strangers or in social settings, you can still adopt behaviors that compel others, subconsciously or not, to be attracted to you.

Charisma is something that you can "switch on" at will. Norma Jean Baker was famous for this ability, and she even named it: "Marilyn." She loved being Marilyn and worked hard to bring her forth with a signature hairstyle, layers of makeup and hours of practice in front of a mirror.

30 http://www.oprah.com/spirit/The-Science-Behind-Charisma-and-Confidence

David Bowie, too, knew how to flip the switch from off duty "David" to flashy "Ziggy Stardust" when it was professionally necessary. With the make-up and switches "off," both celebrities could ride unrecognized on a crowded subway or walk on busy city streets. Most of us don't need to be so grandiose with our charm. The point is, we can all have charisma if we want it badly enough. It's said that Princess Diana, a.k.a. "Shy Di," had to dig deep to project her charismatic self, but she learned how to do it.

Scientists now believe, however, that charisma is a trait that can be cultivated, and they have empirical evidence to prove it.

Here's the trick, using my sister as an example: When you meet Lori for the first time and look into her eyes, you suddenly feel that, to her, you're the most important person in the room. She looks into your eyes, smiles kindly, embraces your hand with both of hers, and seems to genuinely want to know everything about you. She is actively interested in, and focused on you. You sense that she cares about you and is clinging to your every word. She is fully *present* to you in the moment, asking open-ended questions and nodding appreciatively. She leaves you with the feeling that you're fascinating and worthy of knowing. You feel you've known her all your life.

There's also a "calm energy" component to charisma, born of confidence. Scientists[31] have noted that charismatic people speak with a minimum of "ums" and "ahs," and that their speech and physical gestures become more animated when they're speaking. Fun fact: This physicality is called "signaling behavior," gestures that humans made long before the use of language, likely as a means of survival.[32]

Conviction. A person with a strong personal brand speaks and acts with conviction, which is the belief that what you are saying is true. It adds to your credibility, which in turn leads to trust. Humans are hard-wired

31 https://hbr.org/2010/01/defend-your-research-we-can-measure-the-power-of-charisma

32 ibid

to believe most of what they see and hear, especially if a message is delivered convincingly and with conviction. We tend to look up to people who express their beliefs and opinions unwaveringly. People who have strong opinions are attractive to journalists, because opinions matter in a world of truth seekers. The value of a brand increases with the passionate expression of your subject matter expertise.

Commitment to Excellence. A professional with a strong personal brand has demonstrated consistently that she is committed to high standards of integrity and excellence that begins with herself and which has become integrated at the cellular level of her organization. She's communicated this across all of the channels of communication at her disposal, especially through her personal appearance and how she comports herself.

Caring. The strength of your brand is judged by your level of contribution to the communities you serve. Even more important is the level of selfless service and extra value you provide. I call this the "share to shine" principle. It's beautifully illustrated in the book, "The Go-Giver: A Little Story About a Powerful Business Idea," by Bob Burg and John David Mann.[33]

Always think from the customer's perspective and convey messages with their interests in mind. What don't they know about your industry that they should? How can they avoid mistakes? What can you teach them? What is their pain? Give them information they need to make good decisions. Use every opportunity to share your wisdom. One hundred percent of your media messaging should be motivated by a commitment to serve others.

Competence. Talent and track record are major building blocks in the foundation of personal brand and public acclaim. You must be good at what you do—in fact, better than most. Build up your social proof before you step into the media spotlight, i.e., testimonials, endorsements, case studies, customer service track record, audience evaluations, etc. Also, having well-written, optimized online profiles on sites such as LinkedIn,

33 https://www.amazon.com/Go-Giver-Little-Story-Powerful-Business/dp/159184200X

where business professionals hang out, goes a long way in demonstrating your competence.

Authenticity. I've been reading about politicians and political campaigns lately because it's fascinating how candidates are groomed and briefed so they can earn the trust of voters and get themselves elected. Candidates are taught to disguise any number of traits that their constituencies might find objectionable, so we watch candidates kiss babies, go bowling and attend church. They give their publics what the research tells them their publics want. Ironically, authenticity is something you can fake. It's the dark side of branding, and eventually, the spell wears off, and when the public realizes it's been duped, the consequences are severe.

The strength of your brand is judged by your level of contribution to the communities you serve.

When I talk about authenticity, I mean something that is honest and genuine. I don't recommend trying to be anything that you're not. On the contrary—I advocate for finding out who you really are at the core and allowing it to come forth in all its glory, totally uncensored and unrepressed. Take a moment and reflect on some of the people you most admire. Their most striking characteristic is that they seem so comfortable in their own skins, and that they don't seem to give a damn about what other people think. Allow yourself to be authentic, and damn the torpedoes. When you've mastered the art of publicity and your authentic self ripples out in ever-widening concentric circles, your tribe (and everybody has one) will find you.

Let's say, for example, that during the self-research branding exercise mentioned above, that someone says your hairstyle is dorky. You have three options: to go to a stylist and ask for a new look, stick with what you have, or make it even dorkier. Do you think Donald Trump has been criticized? There's a long list of public figures who decided to be authentic by sticking with their actual appearances and even accentuating, because it made them memorable. Pretense is exhausting, and eventually people see through it.

Expertise. Your brand becomes strong simply by virtue of your being an expert. Expertise is inviolate. It's something you've worked hard to acquire and it's in high demand, not only by the media, but by people who need it. Expertise and a strong personal brand make you a publicity powerhouse.

A word about expertise, which you might find interesting because it's extremely effective, is that your expertise needn't necessarily focus on what you do for a profession. It can also be expertise in a hobby or other outside interest that's melded with your professional pursuits. The whole purpose of developing a strong personal brand is that you want to be credible, interesting and attractive to your business target audiences. I've known wealth managers who are also sailing enthusiasts, wine connoisseurs and virtuoso pianists, and these topics and experiences become married to their communications to their clients and prospects. What are your interests? Environmental responsibility? Adventure travel? Working with kids? Aging beautifully? Colorful neckties? All of these can be parlayed into communications and events that attract interest from the media and an audience that's out there waiting to find out about you.

Take the Chapter 12 Quiz

Score 100 percent on every chapter quiz for your chance to win free tuition for the PR Breakthrough™ Publicity Boot Camp:

http://bit.ly/2gqu1XB

Chapter 13

Content Marketing and Brand Journalism

"Content builds relationships. Relationships are built on trust. Trust drives revenue."

— ANDREW DAVIS

There's been so much change in the marketing and public relations worlds. Paradigms are shifting. Terms are being redefined, and traditional, functional lines of responsibility are blurring. Ask 10 different people what "marketing" is, and you'll get 10 different answers. Ask 10 people what PR is, and this, too leads to a variety of responses. Everyone agrees, however, that the new playing field is about earning customer trust by consistently delivering engaging, relevant and valuable content. In other words, a good content strategy builds relationships, and by that very definition, good content strategy *is* public relations. Always has been.

Public relations is concerned with communicating effectively to *all* of an organization's publics, not just potential customers, and not with the sole aim of selling, which is marketing's agenda. Public relations is, and has always been, about "greasing the skids" for sales. It's also given the responsibility for communicating with one, particular public—the media.

Now that advertising is making a slow swan dive into antiquity, or at least, for the time being is being relegated to a less important (or less funded) status until someone cracks the code and makes people pay attention to it again, and that direct marketing is beginning to win gold medals in the "spam" category, marketers are scrambling to adapt to a new way of attracting customers, and they've dubbed it, "content marketing." Others are calling it "brand journalism," a term probably coined by a public relations person. Like the old joke says, "You can call me anything you like—just don't call me late for dinner." Marketing is making a turf grab into PR territory. Regardless, in today's business climate, you can't live without putting valuable content out there. To keep everyone happy, let's henceforth call it "content strategy."

We touched on the importance of content, or rather pounded our fist into it, in Chapter 9, and I described some particular pieces of content that will help you attract media interest, pitch story ideas and include in your brand building activities. In this chapter, we'll veer away from the media audience and talk more about content as a means of providing value, educating and building trust with each of your target audiences.

Content strategy employs many different methods and channels depending upon with which target audience you're communicating. When you prepare your annual communications plan (Chapter 17), you'll define your audience segments and plan their messaging and content strategy accordingly.

Most entrepreneurs and small- to medium-sized businesses find the content marketing process overwhelming, and rightly so. There are so many avenues for getting your content out into the marketplace, and many different kinds of content. Here's a list of the most obvious:

Blogs	eBooks
Newsletters	Reports
InfoGraphics	Presentation Slides

Case Studies	Videos
Social Media	Webinars/Teleseminars
White Papers	Articles
Speeches	Testimonials
Podcasts	Transcripts

You can't do *everything*, especially if it's just you or a handful of staff members, all of whom are wearing many hats. To keep your content strategy manageable, I suggest you focus on one or two items at a time, and leverage them. My friend, Donna Duffy[34], says, "Write it once, then squeeze it dry." This is called, "repurposing" your content.

Just one piece of content, and I'll use your white paper as an example, can be broken apart or re-imagined in many different ways:

* Break it into a series of excerpts, or **snippets,** and post them in social media with a link to your white paper. Snippets can be variations on the title, short statements, quotes and statistics from the content, or brief summary statements of your content.
* Turn your white paper into a **video** and post it on the many video-sharing sites, such as YouTube or Vimeo. Then, do the "snippet" thing and draw traffic to your video through social media.
* If you mentioned other experts or **influencers** in your white paper, reach out to them to let them know that you've done so. Many of them will share your content. If you don't have their email addresses, connect with them on LinkedIn and send an inMail.
* Turn your white paper into a **slide deck**, and upload it to SlideShare. Presentations on SlideShare rank high in search engine results.
* Turn your white paper into a PDF and offer it as a **free download** on your website to capture emails.

34 https://www.pinterest.com/pin/159948224237219674/activity

* Submit your white paper (or an article version of it) to **content communities**. These groups have the potential of spreading your content exponentially. A few of these communities are eZineArticles.com, BlogEngage.com, BizSugar.com, Triberr.com and TribePro.com.
* Use your white paper to secure **speaking engagements**. A well-written white paper goes a long way in establishing your expertise and credibility, and there are many business groups that have an interest in your topic.
* Break your white paper down into several **blog** posts, then direct traffic to your blog via social media.
* There are **paid** ways to distribute your content as well, such as Buzzstream.com and Stumbleupon.com.

As you can see, with just one white paper, you've kept yourself busy for weeks. What's more, if your white paper is evergreen content, it has a long shelf life and you can pull it out next year and execute the same content strategy.

I produce a weekly **podcast** called, "Media Pro Spotlight," which keeps me pretty busy but gives me multiple ways to create and repurpose content while building my brand as a subject matter expert. I have a virtual team that helps me put all the pieces together, as follows:

* I schedule and conduct the interview.
* The MP3 recording of the interview goes to my audio editor, who pieces together the show.
* The recording also goes to a transcribing service.
* The transcription is formatted into a lovely PDF, which is downloadable from the podcast web page on my website.
* I upload the show (via Blubrry) to iTunes.
* My show is then added to the podcast page on my website.
* I announce that the show is on the air via my email list and social media.

* Many shows are recorded in advance, meaning I can schedule the content in advance.
* The show transcripts are collected, edited, and formatted into an eBook, which is promoted as a "free download" from my website, where I collect email addresses.

There are many creative ways to produce content to attract ears and eyeballs to your brand without breaking either the bank or your spirit. One way is to produce a daily (or as often as you can manage), one-minute video of yourself giving a tip, observation or insight. You could record several in one day and schedule them out. Create a YouTube channel, and post the video on your social media channels. I like this tactic for people who are great talkers, but who hate to write.

Public relations is concerned with communicating effectively to all of an organization's publics, not just potential customers, and not with the sole aim of selling.

Use Hootsuite, CoSchedule or some other social media aggregation tool to schedule your posts days or weeks into the future. Automate your delivery process as much as possible. I use Infusionsoft (which is pricey, but powerful) to create automated email campaigns designed to distribute valuable content, nurture prospects, stay in touch with clients, and collect leads.

Always be on the lookout for ways to create content that establishes your expertise and industry leadership. Be patient, yet determined. Make the commitment to keep the content river flowing over the long term. Be aware that most people give up after six months or so, because a good content strategy takes time and effort to sustain and you haven't yet reached the tipping point. If you can stay the course, you're accomplishing what only the elite few can, or will.

Take the Chapter 13 Quiz

Score 100 percent on every chapter quiz for your chance to win free tuition for the PR Breakthrough™ Publicity Boot Camp:

http://bit.ly/2fwopZO

Chapter 14

Smile for the Camera (The Art of the Interview)

"I don't mind doing interviews. I don't mind answering thoughtful questions. But I'm not thrilled about answering questions like, 'If you were being mugged, and you had a light saber in one pocket and a whip in the other, which would you use?'"

—*Harrison Ford*

If your fondest dream is to be a regular guest on national television, radio or podcast talk shows, then your plan should be to develop good interview skills and get lots and lots of practice. If you believe you have the talent and expertise, and if you have a fire in your belly, go for it. Be prepared, however, for the long haul. Hire a professional media trainer, and hone your skills. Rocky had a coach, and you should, too.

It has always been this way: You start in the minor leagues, attracting one follower at a time, speaking for free, honing your skills. At first, you are anonymous, easily forgotten, but you're accumulating some excellent video, audio and print clips, which you're displaying in your website newsroom. And then one day, when you're just about to give up and you're starting to believe that all of this media relations stuff is bull doody, you'll receive an invitation for an interview from some journalist or producer who's on the next highest rung of the ladder—the local morning TV news magazine. Because of your dogged persistence and commitment to learning the craft, you've created word-of-mouth (of which you were unaware). It's slowly becoming known in media circles that you are not only an expert in your field, but that you interview well.

I'm not trying to scare you by telling you that the secret is hard work, determination and persistence. I just want to prepare you. Walking onto a TV set or sitting across the table from a top-tier journalist isn't as easy as people make it look. My first television appearance was years ago with my sister on a local television morning news show. We performed a medley of original songs, and then the host, Steve Baskerville, who's now on CBS 2 Chicago, joined us at the piano and asked us some questions.

His first question was, "So, how long have you two been singing together?" and he put his microphone in front of my mouth, waiting for a gem. As I recall, I babbled incoherently. There were big lights and even bigger cameras pointed at us, and we were totally unprepared for interview questions. Thank goodness there were no iPhones or other ways to capture this interview for posterity, so other than the crew and Steve, (and the thousands of viewers who were watching that fateful, Tuesday morning) there's no evidence. Thankfully, my sister, who's a natural, saved the day and picked up the interview beautifully.

Since that first, humiliating moment on camera, I've dedicated the past three decades training others to step confidently into the media spotlight and thus save themselves from the horrors that unpreparedness can bring. I've learned from my mistakes. You will, too.

This information will be extremely useful for you if you plan to be the official spokesperson for your work. It will also help you if it's your job to prepare others to speak on behalf of your organization.

A Few Basics

You must always be professional in your dealings with the media. It seems a shame I have to say this, but it's shocking to see the level of unprofessionalism through which media professionals must shift on a daily basis. They also get their share of nut jobs. To score points and develop trust, you must demonstrate from the beginning that you are a credible resource and that you understand the media mindset. If you have enough interesting information to share on a consistent basis, you've shown respect for their requirements, and if your personality shines with confidence, then it's inevitable you'll be invited for an interview.

In previous chapters we talked at length about producing great content, e.g., your press kit, case studies and white papers. Having a book is fast becoming a rite of passage, a minimal requirement for anyone seeking a place on the world stage, but it's not absolutely essential if you have an alternative body of work in the form of strong, frequent and relevant content. If you are an author, thought leader or subject matter expert, having a solid content repertoire matters more than I can say. This also holds true if you are preparing your CEO or other high-ranking executive as a spokesperson for your organization. Be sure your organization's press kit, financial performance and reputation are up to snuff.

First, some basics. Eliminate the phrase, **"no comment"** from your vocabulary. I'm hoping you already know this. The temptation to say "no comment" is very high when you or your organization is under scrutiny for an alleged misdeed.[35] "No comment" is a slap in the interviewer's face and brands you as an ignoramus. We'll talk about some alternative things you can say in a moment, but never say "no comment." It's like swearing in front of your grandmother.

A great spokesperson is good at using sound bites, analogies or catchy phrases. A sound bite or analogy helps your audience understand or make sense of a complicated idea or situation. It's also a way to create a "hook"

---

35 See Chapter 17: Dealing with Crisis

that will be associated with you, one that will be often repeated, like the hook in your favorite song. A good one catches on.

Good political speechwriters make it their business to invent show-stopping sound bites and analogies. "Read my lips---no new taxes," is a sound bite delivered in a speech. "Ask not what your country can do for you, ask what you can do for your country," is another.

There were big lights and even bigger television cameras pointed at us, and we were totally unprepared for interview questions.

An example of a good **analogy** is one that was given by Timothy Geitner, who was secretary of the treasury when all hell broke loose with the economy in 2009 and he was being interviewed on camera:

"It's like you're in the cockpit of the plane," he said. "Your engine's burning, smoke's filling the cabin, it's filled with a bunch of people that are fighting with each other about who's responsible, you have terrorists on the plane and people want you to come out of the cockpit and put them in jail. And you have to land the plane. That terrifying core objective in a crisis is to make sure you first put out the fire."

See how he uses an analogy to explain a complicated situation? Listen to TED talks and TV interviews with your favorite thought leaders and notice how they've created sound bites, analogies and catchy phrases to convey their ideas in memorable ways.[36]

Return phone calls or emails from journalists immediately. If they've asked for your help, need information or want to interview you, respond as soon as you can. Always assume they're on deadline. If you don't, or can't, help, say so and explain why. The fact that they reached out to you means that you're on their radar as a resource. Do you like being ignored by journalists and editors when you've asked them for coverage? Of course not. One hand washes the other.

36 http://www.ted.com

Plan, Prepare, Practice

Feature Stories. When you're invited to be interviewed by a journalist, it will often be because you've just sent them a pitch or press release that they really liked, so you'll have a good idea of what they want to talk with you about. ***Tip:*** If, by chance, you miss their call, get back to them *immediately*. If they're on deadline and don't hear right back from you, they'll move on to someone else.

You should plan and prepare for media interviews *before* you send out your press releases or pitches. Think of three key message points that you want to communicate in relation to your announcement, and write them down. Being clear and conversant about your message points keeps you on track and gives you confidence that you're relaying all of the important information you want to convey.

There are times when a reporter hopes he/she can interview you right away, over the phone, which is another good reason to know your three key message points in advance. Most times, however, the journalist will schedule an interview with you, which means you'll have time to prepare.

Take a little time to refamiliarize yourself with the reporter's publication or media outlet so that you understand the audience you're talking to. Also, read or watch the reporter's previous work, if possible, to get a feel for their tone and approach. Are they light-hearted and fun, or serious and fact-based?

When you're setting the interview appointment, ask the journalist or interviewer how or whether you can help them with additional resources for their story, and of course, this depends upon what kind of story this is, but for example, would they like a tour of your facility while they're there? Would they like to meet any other members of your team? Would they like a demonstration of your product? Is there anyone else in the industry they'd like to talk to with whom you can help them connect? It's all about being a good host and being available to help them develop a great story.

If you're being interviewed as a guest for a talk show, the host may provide you with a list of instructions and interview questions. Recently,

I appeared on a talk show that focused on interviews with entrepreneurs. The host sent me detailed instructions on what to wear, when to arrive, what to bring and where to park.

Breaking News Interviews. When a media outlet is doing a feature story about you, because you've sent them a pitch or press release, it's almost always a friendly collaboration between you and the journalist. When the journalist is under deadline pressure, however, and they're calling you on the spur of the moment to get a quote or opinion about a breaking story, it's a different scenario entirely.

I won't get into detail about how to handle a crisis situation here. Crises are different animals and I'll cover those in detail later. Rather, I'm talking about the kind of call you'll get from a journalist who knows you're an expert and needs your expert opinion on short notice.

If the journalist is a warm contact, he may just be calling to ask for your help with the story, and not necessarily because he wants to interview you. He might ask you to tell him where he can find additional information or people to interview. Wow. This is a great relationship. It's always your goal to create this level of trust and partnership with journalists.

The phrase, "no comment," is a slap in the interviewer's face and brands you as an ignoramus.

There are other times when the journalist is calling around to interview three different sources on a story he's writing about a particular industry development. For instance, a reporter who covers the banking industry may have learned about a recent ruling by the FDIC and is calling bank CEOs to ask what impact this ruling will have on banks. The reporter is most likely to call the three CEOs with whom she has already built a level of trust, or who are considered most influential ("big bank" CEOs). Sometimes, though, she'll reach outside this pool of expertise and give some other bank CEO a chance to weigh in on the issue and be quoted in her article.

She'll be very grateful if the CEO is available to talk when she calls. Conversely, she'll be disappointed if the CEO's handlers don't, or won't, put him through right away. Of course, she understands that people are busy, and she may leave a message requesting that the CEO get back to her within a specified time frame. Meanwhile, she'll dial the next CEO on her list, and if she connects and gets the information she needs, then the previous CEO has missed out.

Go over your key messages several times. You wouldn't show up to a piano recital without having practiced your piece a bunch of times, so you wouldn't go into an interview without having practiced being interviewed, either.

If you can, practice with another person. Have them ask you questions that have nothing to do with your subject and practice getting the conversation back on track. Reporters don't try to trick you, but sometimes you wind up getting into a friendly conversation and you want to make sure you can get back to the matter at hand so that the reporter gets all of the important points you wanted to make before you run out of time.

In my weekend media training workshops we get more in depth with what might be considered "tricky" interviews, but most of us entrepreneurs don't have to worry about being blindsided. Our most important task is keeping the interview on track and making sure you make all the important points.

Interview Terminology

There are a few journalistic terms you ought to be aware of. Technically, when you're sitting in an interview with a print journalist, whether in person or over the phone, your entire conversation is "on the record." It's assumed by the reporter that whatever the two of you talk about is okay to be put into his article.

If you say something during the interview that you'd rather he not print, tell him your remark is **"off the record."** I've interviewed many people, and sometimes the conversation strays off topic. It's okay to ask the reporter to keep what you just said, or are about to say, "off the record." He's ethically bound not to put it in his article. You'll rarely, if ever, need to say this if you're being interviewed for a feature or profile.

However, be careful with this one if you or your company is on the spot and the interview is about defending your actions or painting your organization in the most favorable light. In this type of scenario, some reporters don't recognize the words, "off the record." There are cynics out there who will tell you that there's no such thing as off the record. What's supposed to happen after you say, "off the record" is that you can speak freely and honestly during the interview, but the journalist is honor bound not to use the information in his or her story.

Like I said, most interviews you have with journalists won't require you to say, "off the record," but media-trained professionals don't like to take chances. I recently interviewed a powerful woman who had many scandalous stories about a prominent family of industrial giants. She told me a few juicy stories—mostly because I begged—but she insisted that these stories be "off the record." I kept my word. After all, the interview was a flattering feature piece, not investigative journalism.

The next term is, **"not for attribution."** This tells the reporter that it's okay for her to write what you said, but you don't want it to be known that it was you who said it. You'll often hear a TV political reporter say things like, "a source close to the White House said," or "a spokesperson from Enron said." Reporters who cover stories as "watchdogs of the public interest" cultivate and rely upon people who are willing to share information if the reporter promises not to implicate or endanger them in any way. Like I mentioned earlier, journalists need us as much as we need them. What's needed, on both sides, is to establish a bond of trust.

The term, **"on background"** means that, by being interviewed, you're helping a reporter understand a situation better. You're a source of information only. The reporter can't mention or implicate you in any way. The onus on him is to find three other sources who can be quoted, and with your help, he now is better prepared to ask the right questions.

Print Interviews

Many people are reluctant, even afraid, to be interviewed by print journalists. Unless you have something to hide or are under the public microscope for any reason, you should be thrilled at every opportunity to work proactively with the media and get your name in print.

When a reporter visits with you to write a story, first, be glad, and second, relax. My friend, a food and travel writer, interviews some of the top chefs in the industry and shares their inspiring stories in her magazine. She takes lots and lots of notes in a steno pad. Another friend is a health reporter. She uses a digital recorder to capture interviews with family physicians, plastic surgeons and brain surgeons.

Reporters are people, and sometimes they make mistakes. If the story about you has an inaccuracy in it, and it's a mistake in a material fact that might confuse the reader or cause damage to your reputation (your business address, wrong date of your special event, phone number, financial information, etc.), then it's perfectly fine to contact the writer or editor and ask for a correction. Never be rude or angry about it, though. You wouldn't want the editor or reporter to get a bad taste in their mouth about you.

Most publications will make the correction, but just so you know, in most cases, they'll print the correction in a place where no one will see it.

Sometimes, a reporter will ask you a question to which you don't know the answer. Don't try and answer if you don't know. It's perfectly fine to say, **"I don't know,"** but do offer to find the answer and get back to the reporter as soon as you can so she doesn't miss her deadline.

Radio Interviews

Many radio interviews are conducted over the phone or audio-only Skype calls, meaning you can wear sweat pants and a death metal tee shirt if you want. Still, no matter how you're dressed or what your hair looks like, you must prepare for the interview as much or even better than you would if you were being interviewed for print. Why? Because people, undistracted by your looks, are going to hear your voice and what you actually say.

If you do visit the radio studio, the experience might feel a little funny the first couple of times you do it. For one thing, you'll wear headphones and hear your own voice in stereophonic, ultra crisp splendor. It's a bit unnerving at first, but you'll learn to enjoy it.

Assume, always, that the microphone is on. Avoid making any off-hand remarks. If you bring notes to the interview, don't rustle them. Be enthusiastic, and have lots of energy. Make your voice interesting with lots of inflection, speak slowly and clearly, and smile! Your mission is to be entertaining and interesting.

Television Interviews

Every piece of footage of you is valuable for securing additional television interviews and speaking gigs, so practice as if your entire career depended on it. Hire a media trainer to help you if you've never been on camera before. I teach my clients how to sit, how to use their hands and where to look. We role-play each interview, practicing the delivery of key messages and learning how to stay on track. Best of all, we develop his or her on air personality.

Men, wear calf-length socks so that when you cross your legs you're not showing any calf skin. You don't want people looking at your legs instead of your handsome face. If you're a guy whose personal brand is to be clean-shaven, be sure to shave before your on-camera appearance, because for some reason, stubble really shows up. If having an unshaved look is part of your brand, then skip the shave.

Women, avoid wearing solid black or white. Some shows use black or white backgrounds, and you don't want to blend into the walls. TV studios use bright lights to illuminate their sets, so avoid wearing jewelry that might reflect the light. And, don't wear too much make-up. If you're lucky, there will be a make up artist on set who will make sure you look good under the lights, but if there isn't, keep your make-up simple.

Try to get "um" out of your vocabulary. When you're speaking to a group or on camera, your "ums" are distracting. It takes the listener out of your story. Train yourself not to say "um."

Jan Fox, whose book[37] teaches you everything you need to know to be on camera, suggests this exercise: Have someone ask you, "What's the last thing you did last night?"

Don't talk! Think first. When you know what you're going to say, start talking, but be careful—you're about to say "um." It always happens. So shut your mouth again, and think it through. Then finish your answer. Do this exercise often. It's a fun game at the dinner table or at parties.

Enthusiasm and cheerfulness are key during a TV interview. Get yourself psyched. You need to be extra animated in front of the camera. Videotape yourself some time, or have someone videotape you, and see how you come across. Because I'm a natural introvert, I used to think I was going way overboard when I was on camera, now I'm more comfortable being "on." You will, too, the more you do it.

Look at the person who is interviewing you, not at the camera. Never look at the camera. You can look occasionally at the studio audience, if there is one, when they laugh at your joke. The camera doesn't exist, as far as you know.

And finally, don't let the interview go sideways. If you have a good rapport with the interviewer, it's easy to fall into a pleasant conversation about something that has nothing to do with any of the messaging you prepared. You're there to talk about your messaging, not about last night's Grammy Awards. You simply don't have the time. Develop your skills in bringing the conversation back around to your topic.

Satellite & Radio Tours

Satellite media tours (SMTs) are a series of back-to-back, live television or video interviews, usually in four-hour sessions (8:00 a.m. to noon) and about five minutes apart, depending on how many interviews you schedule. Truth be told, you have little chance of booking SMTs in major markets unless you are an "A list" celebrity, high-ranking politician or all-star

37 http://foxtalks.com/product/get-yourself-on-tv-what-to-do-when-you-get-there/

athlete. If you're not (yet), stick with network affiliates' morning shows, and try to target as many markets as possible. Start locally.

SMTs can be conducted in a studio, but are best in an interesting location that illustrates your topic and has visual appeal. For example, if you're a chef or nutrition expert, having a kitchen as your backdrop is nice. I've done SMTs in animal shelters, back stage at the ballet, in front of a lion cage and at the airport.

You have the option of using a green screen in the studio, where they can drop in a background that fits the subject matter. It's common to see an interview with a politician who appears to be seated outside the Capitol Building.

Your story needs a strong news hook and a well-trained expert or spokesperson. The types of stories you'd pitch for SMTs might include:

* Seasonal stories, such as back-to-school, preparing for winter, keeping your pet safe during 4th of July, holiday recipes how to plant flower bulbs
* Advice-related stories, like how to travel with your pet, how to avoid mosquito bites, how to plant flower bulbs, how to organize your office
* Expert analysis of breaking news stories
* Feature stories, e.g., remarkable achievement by local resident, national recognition of a local child
* Stories with broad consumer appeal
* Announcements of a huge local event

Take the Chapter 14 Quiz

Score 100 percent on every chapter quiz for your chance to win free tuition for the PR Breakthrough™ Publicity Boot Camp:

http://bit.ly/2fhbcsC

Chapter 15

Gripes, Pet Peeves and Horror Stories

"I don't have pet peeves like some people. I have whole kennels of irritation."

—WHOOPI GOLDBERG

Previously, I've pointed out some of the things that you should *not* do when you're wearing your publicity or content marketing hat. Now, I'm going to pull out all the stops, because by showing you what's wrong, you will be more likely to know what's right. It's my goal with this book to help you become a polished and professional publicity practitioner, or at least, to know what a good one does and is up against.

Following is a list of the behaviors I've seen from people who have acknowledged that they need assistance with public relations, media relations, corporate communications, publicity and content marketing, but who haven't yet acquired a sophistication of the processes involved. As a result, they unwittingly sabotage themselves by making big mistakes, such as:

You don't return calls or emails from journalists. I don't know why people fail to do this. Maybe it's a symptom of a general lack of common courtesy. Maybe whoever's in charge has a pathological fear of the media. Maybe the person in charge of the PR function is unqualified for the position. Maybe it's all of the above. I've witnessed all of these things during my career, but as in most cases, the belief in the value of positive press coverage rolls down from the top.

I have a friend who's a senior editor for a two-million-circulation lifestyle magazine. On Monday, she reached out to the PR people at three separate hotel properties to make arrangements for site tours and interviews with their executive chefs. Her deadline was Friday. Not one of people she contacted returned her call. She wrote to me, baffled, asking me, "What's wrong with PR people?"

You don't have an online press kit or a description of your company on your website. Once I was asked by the local newspaper to write a 100-word descriptive blurb about 20 separate businesses, each of which had been named "best" in their categories in the annual "best of" competition. I had a one-week deadline, which seemed generous.

The first thing I did was check each business's website to find its online press kit. None of the 20 had one. Next, I searched for their "about us" section, and the paragraph that would give me exactly what I needed, i.e., the who, what, when, where and why of the business—their boilerplate. I struck out again. Not one of these 20 businesses had a concise description of themselves on their websites. So far, I'd spent about three hours searching for information that ought to easily have been found.

None of these 20 businesses had a concise description of themselves on their websites.

The only other option I had was to call each place of business, so I clicked the "contact" tab on their websites. None of them provided a contact email address, and only five of them listed a phone number. A few provided a form on the contact page that required filling out. I wasn't going to do that. That meant I'd need to spend time doing additional research to locate phone numbers. The rest I called. Five of them answered the phone and were very pleasant and accommodating. I left recorded voice mail messages for six of them, and of the remaining nine, people who were not the managers or business owners answered the phone, put me on hold, came back on the line and took a message. By Wednesday, none of them had called me back, so I had to call all of them again. On Friday, my deadline day, I had to call several of them a third time.

Remember, I wasn't calling them to sell vacuum cleaners or rat them out on "60 Minutes." I was calling to facilitate their being honored and getting great publicity for having been voted "the best" by their peers. If a business isn't equipped or willing to respond to these kinds of opportunities, their prognosis is poor for long-term survival.

You blast your press releases to every outlet, every time, indiscriminately. If you listen to the Media Pro Spotlight podcast, you'll hear that this is a common gripe among media professionals. The typical journalist receives up to 300 emails a day, and most of them are press releases that they consider "spam," because the sender went for the shotgun approach. Healthcare editors get press releases about auto repair. Business editors get press releases about food recipes. You get the idea. Be fastidious about the creation and segmentation of your media lists.

You don't do your research before pitching a journalist. This one's related to the previous gripe about people who spread their press releases like manure. It's a best practice to pitch your stories to one journalist at a time, after having done the research to learn more about the journalist's interests, style, previous work and contact preferences. It shows respect, and that you're a professional. No one likes having their time wasted, and having to sift through piles of email that's mostly irrelevant. It's annoying and frustrating. Hacks and novices are in the majority, so your effort to do things right goes a long way.

All of the rules of courtesy and professionalism that we show to customers and prospects are the same we show with journalists. We lead by earning trust and providing value.

Your press releases are poorly written or improperly formatted. I only mention this because my media friends bring it up all the time. "You wouldn't believe the stuff I get," is a common complaint. It's too tempting for journalists and editors to hit the "delete" button these days because of the sheer volume of unprofessional submissions they get every day, so if they do open your press release, you want it to shine. If you're consistently on the mark, they'll be less trigger-happy the next time they see emails from you.

Your press releases are purely promotional or not newsworthy. There are people who think that the press release is an opportunity to promote or advertise. It's not. In fact, it's highly inappropriate to try. Resist the urge to sneak in sales messages. The press release is a news story, or an announcement of something noteworthy, an important event that's about to happen. The minute an editor spots a sales agenda—poof! It's deleted. Want to advertise something? Call their advertising department.

You don't deliver what you say you were going to deliver. A writer friend of mine traveled to a foreign country to do a story about a lovely travel destination. He arrived at the arranged location promptly at the designated time (on a Saturday), and was puzzled that there was no one there to greet him and show him around. There was no one on site who knew what was going on, so he called the media contact person's cell phone. It went to voice mail. He called several times. Then, he called his editor in New York, who did some digging and learned that the media contact was out on vacation. My friend wrote the story anyway, but it left a bad taste in his mouth.

Another friend, a television news producer, was pitched by a person who promised to give the news crew a backstage pass to an important political event. When the crew arrived on location, they were denied access because the person who pitched the story had failed to follow through.

Keep your promises. Don't say you can definitely arrange something when there's a possibility it will fall through. Show up when you say you will. Answer your cell phone if you're the listed media contact.

You're a pest. Relentless follow-up is appropriate in some situations, but it's not okay to harangue a newsroom. If you've sent a press release that pertains to an upcoming event or is a story in which you have strong confidence, then it's okay to call a day or so after you've sent your pitch or press release to ask whether your media contact received it. It's possible your item was inadvertently missed.

The press release is a news story, or an announcement of something newsworthy, or an important event that's about to happen.

It's also possible that your media contact is not interested in your item or can't use it for any number of reasons. Perhaps they've already written a similar story that week, or their news crew is booked up, or your topic doesn't fit into their programming, or they're just not interested, period. If the media contact doesn't return your call or respond to your email, then let it go. Don't call day after day after day. Not only does it drive them underground where you're concerned, but it brands you as a nuisance.

When I was a newbie in the public relations agency business, it was my main job to secure media coverage for clients who were paying monthly retainers of $10,000 or more. "I want ink!" screamed my bosses. Under this kind of pressure, agency PR pros are obliged to follow up every single press release and be held accountable for the results. Not all press releases, however, are follow-up worthy, because as exciting as the content of the press release might be to the client, there's no guarantee that the media will be able to, or want to, pick it up. It's a big can of worms and a stomach-twisting complication.

Therefore, it's extremely important that you have realistic expectations for any of the pitches or news releases you issue. There is no guarantee of coverage, ever, but coverage is lovely when you get it and much more valuable to you than any marketing campaign. What's needed is to keep trying with new material. Have patience, and don't be a pest. PR people who have worked as journalists know this. Listen to them.

You think that because you have purchased advertising with the media outlet that they're obliged to write a story about you. [Sound of air being sucked inward through teeth.] In the traditional media world, there is a giant barrier, called the "Chinese Wall," between the editorial and advertising departments. In the editorial department are journalists with a sacred trust and an inviolate code of ethics. They report the objective truth, and cannot be bought. To even suggest such an idea is an insult of the highest magnitude.

If you want guaranteed media coverage, you must pay for it. If it's absolutely crucial that your chosen audience get exposed to your messaging, buy a full-page ad with your message in big, bold letters. Big corporations do this all the time. They can afford to.

There are exceptions, of course, to every rule. There's a thing called, "checkbook journalism," or "pay for play editorial." In most communities are local "magazines" that are chock full of articles about local businesses, but it's all paid editorial. Every feature story is actually an advertorial. Also, national trade magazines often will write an article about you as reward for your having signed a long-term advertising contract or have purchased their cover spot. Most of the clients I work with don't have the budget to sustain this kind of paid editorial coverage for long.

If you purchase an ad with a traditional media outlet, however, do not expect in-kind editorial consideration. The editorial department is not connected with the advertising department. They are mutually exclusive.

There are actually people out there who will send out a press release and demand coverage from the editor, even if the story isn't strong or pertinent, because they're advertisers. This is an awful mistake if the editor is a classically trained journalist.

You ask to see a story before it's written. Unfortunately, you can't control the substance of a story or what is said about you, unless the story is an advertorial and you have paid the media outlet to have a copywriter (not reporter) write a flattering profile on your behalf. If you ask the reporter who's interviewing you if you can see the story before it goes to print, he or she will give you a sad, embarrassed smile and explain politely that it doesn't work that way. You will see the story after it appears.

Remember, we live in the United States, a nation that protects the freedom of the press from censorship by the government or other special interests. The press, in turn, strives for factual accuracy and unbiased reporting. The very reason the press has a sacred obligation to be objective and truthful is why a story about you in the media carries such positive weight and value. People are inclined to believe what they read or hear from journalists, so if they talk about you at all, it's implied that you're important and credible.

It is extremely rare that any article written about you will do harm to your reputation if you are a business that operates with integrity. Only the largest of organizations and public figures, who receive the greatest amount of public scrutiny and have the greatest impact on society, need to mind their ps and qs where interaction with the media is concerned. These entities pay millions to keep public relations professionals on retainer to be proactive in protecting their positive images and maintaining the two-way flow of communication with the media.

You complain to the editor after the story is published because it paints you in a bad light. A restaurant critic has written a bad review about you. A banking reporter has said he was unable to "reach you for comment" when a customer complained about allegedly having been denied for a mortgage loan based on his/her race, creed or status. A review of your latest gizmo by a journalist was unfavorable. You received a poor book review from an important blogger.

Take this type of experience as an opportunity to improve your service, your response time to media inquiries, your product's functionality or your writing skills. Do not place blame on the reporter or the media outlet that ran the story. Most important, do not complain to the media outlet. Instead, move on with your life. One bad review or well-publicized customer complaint isn't going to ruin you. Whining does nothing but confirm a weak character in the media's eyes. It indicates an inability to take responsibility for one's own actions.

There is no guarantee of coverage, ever, but coverage is lovely when you get it and much more valuable to you than any advertising campaign.

Again, there are exceptions to every rule. If there were egregious errors in the reported facts, or you have compelling evidence to suggest the reporter's sources were unreliable or had axes to grind (e.g., a disgruntled former employee), then you have the right to raise your concerns with the editor or producer who green-lighted the story. This *must* be a civil discussion, and you must walk into it showing respect as you would to any other professional with whom you have built a relationship of trust. Showing respect earns respect.

Would you be recompensed in any way in the form of a retraction, apology or a new story? Perhaps, perhaps not. It's your grace in the situation that matters. Always take the high road, even if your gut is twisting, because in the long run, the high road serves you best.

You're a diva. A diva is a person who has lost sight of respect and concern for others. If you want to act as a diva when a reporter is doing a story about you, then the journalist may not be kind when writing your story and paint you in an unfavorable light. Good writers "show," not "tell." She won't say, "Gosh, that guy's a jerk." Instead, she'll paint a word picture: "Johnny Diva screamed at the waiter to bring him a clean fork, then blew a waft of cigarette smoke into his face."

Don't make demands on media people, or treat them, or anyone in your entourage, as inferior beings. It won't bode well for you, career-wise. Once you're branded as a "jerk," it's hard to climb back.

You have unrealistic expectations. When you employ media relations and publicity as strategies to build your brand, awareness and mailing list, expect to be in it for the long haul. To expect immediate results is—unrealistic.

Not every story you submit for consideration will be picked up. Not every publicity campaign will resonate with your audience or sell tickets. Even though a news crew has added you to its day book to cover your event, it doesn't mean they'll be there, because they may be diverted to a four-alarm fire instead.

The press is the same as any other target audience with which you communicate regularly. Not every prospect is ready to buy, right? You reach out to them, introduce yourself, provide value, establish trust and nurture the relationship until the day they finally decide to pull the trigger. Sometimes, you'll hit a home run. Most of the time, though, it's approaching each day with patience and persistence. The press helps you achieve your objectives in concert with all of the other things you're doing to create and sustain a successful business. Publicity is a powerful tool. Your only expectation for it is that it requires conscientious application over the long term by someone who knows how to wield it, whether it's you or someone to whom you assign the responsibility.

The press helps you achieve your objectives in concert with all of the other things you're doing to create and sustain a successful business.

Your website is unfriendly to journalists, and/or your online presence is lacking. I can tell many stories about journalists who were thwarted from their interest in doing a story because they couldn't get what they needed from the target's website. No contact information… no press kit… no company description… amateurish or antiquated website design… poorly written content. Today it's common that rather than calling you outright, a journalist will research you first by conducting an Internet search on you or your business. If your online presence is lacking, it's a big red flag that you're not a respected expert. What kind of business professional *still* doesn't have a decent LinkedIn profile? Why does nothing come up in the google search? Why does your website look like a crazy quilt? Where's your CEO—in hiding? Reporters want to talk to credible resources and experts who are in touch with the world. A poor website proves that you're not.

Your website's "press room" is merely an archive of previous press coverage you've received. It's lovely that you have PDFs and videos of previous press coverage. It validates you as a credible resource. Certainly these things should be available for viewing on your website. But since the press room is intended as a place where journalists can go to become educated on your business, there needs to be more up there than viewing the press releases and video clips in your archives. They're not your Mom, watching every second of your footage and beaming with pride. Do yourself and your business a favor by investing in the creation of an online press kit.

You use social media only to sell and brag about accomplishments, not to engage. There are many organizations and people out there who use social media as a place to post company announcements and press releases. It's called, "humble bragging," and most of your audience recognizes it for what it is. Few will be impressed. They do not engage with their followers. They do not write or share content that is useful to their intended audiences, and if they do, their agenda is to sell. All they do is promote, promote, promote. At the strategic level, they never asked themselves, "What is the strategic value of having a presence on Pinterest/Facebook/Snapchat/LinkedIn/Twitter/Channel du Jour?" You need to understand the value and impact of all of your channels of communication. Know exactly who you're talking to, and then deliver value. Educate. Entertain. Inspire. Stop blasting your followers with self-congratulatory, boring boasting. Believe me, nobody's listening, except your competition.

You replace all traditional communications strategy with social media. There are many reasons organizations have done this, i.e., have abandoned traditional communications strategies and jumped on board the social media train, thinking (and hoping, because social media is cheap) social media will do the whole job of building brand. But beware! The Internet is flooded with content, and its impact and effectiveness are in decline. Anyone with an Internet connection can produce content. Use a mix of strategies and tactics to build awareness and establish trust for your business. Be present in all of the places where your audience is.

You avoid social media altogether, because you don't see the value. It's appalling that there are *still* C-suite executives, subject matter experts and business development professionals who have empty, or non-existent LinkedIn profiles, and 10 or fewer connections. There is enormous strategic value in having a presence in the digital space if there's any chance your audiences are in there, too. It's how you are vetted by your primary, secondary and tertiary audiences. When journalists are looking for experts to interview, they go to LinkedIn and check you out. When investors want to know who's at the helm of your organization, they look on LinkedIn. Many journalists and potential customers look on Twitter, too, to see what you've posted. If you're in an industry that continues to regard social media as taboo, or more foolishly, as a fad, then you're leaving money and brand awareness on the table.

Take the Chapter 15 Quiz

Score 100 percent on every chapter quiz for your chance to win free tuition for the PR Breakthrough™ Publicity Boot Camp:

http://bit.ly/2fClRN9

Chapter 16

Dealing with Crisis

"Then the shit hit the fan."

—*John Kenneth Galbraith*

Crisis is a shock to the system. It hits you when you least expect it—fire, scandal, management malfeasance, slander, cyber crime, workplace violence, frivolous lawsuits—and just like that, your world is turned upside down and the blood drains out of your face.

Before a crisis occurs, *if* it occurs, you should have put time and effort into building a good reputation. The stronger your reputation is before a crisis, the better you'll fare in the court of public opinion. A good reputation is a force field. It's not impervious, but it's better than being naked and unarmed.

W. Timothy Coombs says a crisis is "a significant threat to operations or reputation that can have negative consequences if not handled properly."[38] A crisis is publicity's evil twin. It's when public opinion and media attention take a sudden, aggressive turn against you. A crisis is *newsworthy,* dang it, but it doesn't have to mean it's the end of the world.

38 http://www.instituteforpr.org/crisis-management-communications/

You can *plan and prepare* for it and be armed and ready if barbarians crash the gates.

Large organizations have in place crisis contingency plans that spell out, in great detail, how they intend to operate in the event of a disaster. They create a crisis management team (CMT), usually comprising C-suite executives and heads of public relations, legal, security, operations, IT, finance and human resources, to create a crisis management plan. Every contingency is explored and addressed, no matter how unlikely a scenario seems. A big business, for example, will have a plan in place should an act of God knock out the power grid and computer operations are compromised.

Maybe you're not a large organization with a staff to man the lifeboats and a team of lawyers to bail you out, but observing how the big companies plan for and handle crisis is instructive for all of us. The Titanic, for example, is a lesson for us all. The launch got great publicity, but when push came to shove, they sacrificed public safety for bragging rights, and there was no "Plan B."

A crisis contingency plan considers the protection of human life, first and foremost. It must also plan for the mitigation of financial loss and reputational damage. The CMT pre-drafts messages, trains and prepares employees and conducts exercises to practice and work out the bugs. Think "fire drill." The plan is updated annually, at the least.

While you may not need to have a 200-page crisis contingency plan in your bottom left hand desk drawer, you should still think through all of the scenarios that could cause harm to your business operations and reputation. Hopefully, you have insurance, a strong set of legal documents and technical support. But like the large organizations that have an in-house team of skilled public relations pros, you, too, should have a *written* crisis communications plan to help you keep a clear head and react appropriately.

Why a written crisis communications plan (CCP)? Because when bullets are flying over your head you may, as Egon says in the movie, "Ghostbusters," be "terrified beyond the capacity for rational thought." When you're blinded by panic or bloodlust, your CCP will be the voice of reason. In it, you've written out your key messages, templates for press releases and detailed instructions for communicating with your stakeholders.

Following are some foundational concepts about crisis communications to aid you during your planning process. All of this information has been time tested and adopted as best practice.

Be First, Fast, Correct and Consistent

Suppose there's been an incident that's destroyed property or has resulted in death or injury. You must act swiftly. People, including the media and stakeholders, want to know what's going on, and the first thing they'll do is consult the Internet. This is why you prepare in advance. (See "Communications Channels" below.)

Research shows that a crisis does less reputational damage if the organization is *first* to report the crisis, ideally within the first hour after the crisis occurs. It's crucial that you tell your side of the story before anyone else can. The media, too, strive to be first and fast on breaking news stories, and on the scene, they'll interview any witnesses they can find. Witnesses, unfortunately, aren't always on your side. Adding to the complication is that everyone, even the old lady down the street, has a phone with a video camera, so being first and fast with a story and managing the messaging, whether it's you or the media, is a competitive sport.

Talk to the media before anyone else can. Don't be silent! You need to be the one controlling the story. You never know what other people are going to say, or what their motivations are. The information they relay could be wrong, and some might see it as an opportunity to attack you. By telling your story first, you are, in PR industry parlance, "stealing thunder."

Remember the game, "Whisper Down the Lane?" We'd play it in elementary school. The teacher had us form a big circle around the classroom, and she'd whisper something to the child next to her. That child would whisper the same message to the child beside him, and so on, around the entire circle. The last child would then say out loud the message he'd been given. Invariably, the message was different than the one the teacher started around the circle. The game demonstrates that human recollection is unreliable. The intent of the exercise was to show us that rumors and gossip are likely untrue and ought not to be spread.

W. Timothy Coombs says a crisis is, "a significant threat to operations or reputation that can have negative consequences if not handled properly."

There have been organizations in the past that have kept their heads in the sand, hoping the furor would die down over time and life would go on as usual. What happens, though, is that when word gets out that the organization knew about a problem and didn't report it, people assume that the organization doesn't care about their safety. For example, there have been cases in auto manufacturing when management knew about certain defects but didn't tell anyone about them. Word got out—it always does. In any case, the damage you do to yourself by keeping the news to yourself is far, far worse than if you'd told the truth from the very beginning.

Before going public, double-check all the facts to ensure your information is accurate. You don't want to risk losing credibility in times of crisis, because humans are irrational and many will lash out if they do not trust you. You don't want to risk being perceived as incompetent.

As an organization, you must speak with one voice. Keep your team well informed of the facts, and be on point with your messaging. Everyone needs to sing from the same sheet music.

Be Authentic: Admit, Apologize and Sympathize

The story of the 1982 Tylenol crisis is in public relations textbooks as one of the finest examples of a well-handled crisis situation *ever*.[39] They were first, they were fast, and their primary concern was the public safety.

39 http://iml.jou.ufl.edu/projects/fall02/susi/tylenol.htm

Rather than doing irreparable harm to their brand, they took their place in history as a brand with integrity. They stood by their credo:

> *We believe our first responsibility is to the doctors, nurses and patients, to mothers and fathers and all others who use our products and services.*[40]

There have been organizations throughout history that attempt to downplay or hide the truth about the harm they or their employees have caused, the accusations of whistleblowers, industrial accidents or the depth of financial misdeeds. It's this lack of ethics that have earned public relations professionals an unsavory reputation as "spin doctors." It's assumed that our job is to take the truth and twist it to our client's advantage, an act of complicity with corporate psychosis. Unfortunately, a few bad apples have spoiled it for the whole bunch.

In actuality, public relations practitioners stand for telling the truth and taking the high road in all situations. We hold a high standard and keep it aloft by repeating the litany of PR's mission, which is to build and maintain mutually beneficial relationships that are based on trust and in service to others. Doing so requires authenticity and operating according to the organization's mission and values.

As the title of this book suggests, PR is an art form that rides on the back of years of scientific exploration and painstaking research. And, in my opinion, some of the most fascinating demonstrations of artistic PR are CEO apologies. A great CEO apology is a thing of beauty.

In the advent of a crisis situation, it's best practice to make a public apology. Patrick Doyle, president of Dominoes USA, delivered an apology on YouTube[41] after a couple of employees in Conover, North Carolina, uploaded a prank video that went viral. Doyle's PR team obviously understands the concept of immediacy, and that people consult the internet *first* to access information and discover the truth.

---

40 http://www.jnj.com/sites/default/files/pdf/jnj_ourcredo_english_us_8.5x11_cmyk.pdf

41 http://bit.ly/1MStDsi

With a public apology, you are admitting the problem exists and taking responsibility for the situation. Explain how the situation occurred. Try and limit the scope of the problem if you can. An example of this is, "This is the first time anything like this has ever happened." Explain what steps you will take to rectify the situation, i.e., the solution you will implement or the safeguards you will put in place.

If people were physically hurt or killed as the result of an incident for which you or your organization are responsible, or were harmed otherwise by financial loss, property damage or evacuation, it is vital that you express concern and sympathy for these victims. Otherwise, you risk being perceived as a monster and the public tide will turn against you. When a company is in reaction mode and stress is at its peak, everyone's doing their best to implement the plan and restore operations. It's easy to forget to tell people that one, simple thing: that you care, and that you're doing something about it.

How to be a Spokesperson

Talk about being in the hot seat! This important role should be assigned to someone who's trained and prepared to interact with, and report to, the media during a crisis. This isn't always the person in charge of public relations. Ideally, it's your CEO or an expert in a leadership position. It's PR's role to prepare your spokesperson and keep them on point 24/7.

Get media training for your spokespeople, or for yourself if you expect to be the person in charge of interacting with the media. When you're in crisis mode, it's not a time to "wing it." The pressure of lights, camera, and a microphone in your face is not for amateurs. If you've watched competent spokespeople on the evening news and thought what they were doing looked easy, think again. Even if you're a natural, there's much you need to know and learn. Here are some examples of the techniques you're taught in media training:

- Avoid the phrase, "no comment." It implies you're guilty, or that you're hiding something. It's also considered uncouth.

* Speak clearly, and use language everyone can understand. Don't use jargon or industry terms. Use analogies to explain difficult concepts. If people can't understand what you're saying, they'll think you're being deliberately confusing because you're hiding something.
* Have a calm demeanor, and make strong eye contact. Practice, practice and practice some more to eliminate the use of "ums" and "ahs" from your speech, and to learn not to fidget or pace when you're nervous. When you stammer or look nervous, people think you are being deceptive.

Communication Channels

When crafting your crisis communications plan, your primary focus should be on how you'll deliver key information to stakeholders, not how you'll handle the media. Your goal during a crisis is to use all of the communications channels at your disposal to inform and update your publics fast, e.g., social media, website, intranet, press releases and mass notification systems like text, email and automated voice mail.

People react differently to the same message depending on what channel it's delivered on. It's called the "channel effect." The medium is the message. The crisis communications plan will list all of the channels you will use and how your messages will be presented on each. As much as is possible, you will draft template messages so that all that's needed when you're in full alert is to fill in the blanks or tweak slightly.

Research shows that a crisis does less reputational damage if the organization is first to report the crisis, ideally within the first hour after the crisis occurs.

Take a hard look at your ***website.*** If you're with a large organization, it's likely to be the first place people will go to get information during a crisis. Some companies opt for creating a separate website to which people are directed immediately after the crisis occurs. Many experts recommend using your main website's home page as the information center. Whichever choice you make, strive for ease of use. It should be glaringly obvious to visitors the minute they enter your site where to find the information they're looking for.

If you are a large organization with an ***intranet*** or ***enterprise social networking*** site, assign someone to manage and monitor it. Employees are your greatest assets during a crisis. When they're pre-trained, fully informed and kept in the loop, they are your greatest ambassadors. Ensure your customer-facing and customer service personnel understand their roles, what messages to convey, and to whom they should direct media inquiries. Employees' roles during a crisis should be clearly spelled out in the ***employee handbook*** as well.

In the past, it was common for companies to hold ***press conferences*** to make official statements, release information and to answer journalists' questions. These events get key journalists in the same room at the same time, meaning fewer individual interviews will have to be done with your spokesperson. But beware—you must be prepared, rehearsed and ready for a barrage of questions. Reporters can be unexpectedly aggressive or hostile, depending on your reputational track record. The crisis team should make a list of all possible questions that might be asked and the spokesperson(s) must rehearse the answers and know them cold. Stick to your message points. If you don't yet have all of the facts, say so. Watch this video of Secretary of State Donald Rumsfeld briefing the media the day of the September 11, 2001 terrorist attacks: https://youtu.be/wXuSWOmnP7Q.

Mass notification systems are those that allow you to alert many people at once with a recorded, email, social media or text message. They're especially useful when public safety is an ongoing concern, i.e., during or after a flood, earthquake, forest fire, bridge collapse, etc. The message provides a brief overview of the crisis and provides instructions on what actions to take and directs people to an additional resource, such as a website address or toll-free number.

Social Media Crisis

Crisis communications expert Jonathan Bernstein lists several ways that a social media crisis can rear its ugly head via social media:

* By a disgruntled customer who went online to post his grievances, and his complaints went viral
* By a disgruntled employee
* By a "key influencer" who has a burr under his saddle about a particular topic
* By an alleged news event "going viral" — even if later it turned out to be fake news

"A social media crisis is a crisis in the traditional sense, because in the 21st Century, social media has become 'traditional media,'" says Bernstein. "If what is happening seriously hurts, or could hurt, an individual's or organization's reputation—its most important asset—then it's a crisis. Economic loss (to the alleged offender) usually goes right along with it, exacerbating the crisis."

There are four different kinds of publics who use social media channels in a crisis:[42] (1) The people (creators and influencers) who post information about a crisis to inform the stakeholders; (2) the social media followers who consume this information from the creators; (3) people who aren't active in social media, but get their facts via word of mouth from the people who are; and (4) trolls.[43]

Scan your social media channels regularly so you can spot when people are chatting about you. You need to be aware of these conversations

42 http://www.instituteforpr.org/crisis-management-communications/

43 In Internet slang, a troll is a person who sows discord on the Internet by starting arguments or upsetting people, by posting inflammatory, extraneous, or off-topic messages in an online community with the deliberate intent of provoking readers into an emotional response or of otherwise disrupting normal on-topic discussion, often for their own amusement. (Wikipedia)

so that you can step in to diffuse any negativity early and fix problems. Be aware of the rumors, and try to reverse them if you can, but not on social media. Other channels are better for this: op-ed pieces, your blog, letters to the editor, and if the rumor is particularly damaging, in a press conference.

Don't get emotional; remain calm. Assess the situation to find the origin of it. Get the facts straight. There are trolls out there who chime in sometimes to stir up discord or spread gossip. People are generally good at spotting trolls, and if you have a good reputation, their nonsense won't be taken too seriously.

If, however, you sense that a consumer complaint is legitimate, you must fix the problem as soon as possible. Respond with transparency, respect and caring, and take the conversation off line. Never engage in a public battle.

The Aftermath

In the post-crisis phase, business is returning to normal and you are no longer front-page news. This is a time for reflection and analysis. Keep a record of what worked well, and what didn't.

If the crisis was severe and required corrective action on your part, provide frequent updates via your blog, Twitter, emails, YouTube videos and mass notifications, not to reflect back and relive what happened, but to describe improvements in process, repairs that were made and to praise those who pitched in.

Irreparable Harm

Sometimes, the damage to a brand is so severe that there's no way to recover. In that case, there's no other option but to start from scratch and do what's necessary to rebuild trust. Can this be done? Has anyone ever emerged from a career-killing scandal and reclaimed their good reputations? Yes, but it's difficult. We've all watched celebrity careers rise and fall. Celebrity or not, none of us is immune from the ravages of reputational destruction, and the consequences are cruel. I've known people who had to move to another part of the country, switch professions and change their names.

Life changes on a dime, so be on your toes—prepared, rehearsed and humble. As Warren Buffet said, "It takes 20 years to build a reputation and five minutes to ruin it. If you think about that, you'll do things differently."

Do You Really Have a Crisis on Your Hands?

All that having been said, how do you decide whether a situation is a crisis and requires an immediate, proactive response? Are there times when you should just let things be? What happens, for example, if you discover that there are negative perceptions of you by a certain group, or that your reputation *might* be in danger because of a recent incident of poor customer service, or that your CEO has been rumored to have been involved in scandalous behavior? Here are four possible actions you could take.

One is, you do nothing. You've thought it through, and you realize that this is something that will pass. You've decided you may be overreacting and you're making way more of a big deal out of it than anyone in the outside world would.

The story of the 1982 Tylenol crisis is in public relations textbooks as one of the finest examples of a well-handled crisis situation ever.

Two is, you do something, but only if you absolutely have to. Your attorney might have advised you to keep hush-hush about an issue, because calling attention to it might make it worse, legally or otherwise. I have a friend who is the general manager of a prestigious golf club. Very tragically, a little girl wandered onto the property during the night, unobserved by her parents, fell into one of the golf course water features, and drowned. What do you do in a situation like this? We took a "wait and see" approach. The general manager did all she could to cooperate with the authorities as they investigated the tragedy, and we prepared an official statement should any of the local media outlets call with questions, but we did not proactively reach out to the media. As it turns out, the situation was resolved and the GM was never contacted by journalists to make a statement.

Three is, do something *before* a problem arises. This is the proactive solution. If you know, for example, that at 12 noon on Saturday your computer system is going to be down for upgrades, then it is proactive of you to inform in advance everyone who might be affected.

The fourth strategy is to call in others to help you resolve an issue. An obvious application of this strategy is in the case of a natural disaster when several entities join together to provide aid and assistance.

Take the Chapter 16 Quiz

Score 100 percent on every chapter quiz for your chance to win free tuition for the PR Breakthrough™ Publicity Boot Camp:

http://bit.ly/2fFqC8F

Chapter 17

The Communications Plan

"When you establish a destination by defining what you want, then take physical action by making choices that move you towards that destination, the possibility for success is limitless and arrival at the destination is inevitable."

— *Steve Maraboli*

If you've never gone through the exercise of creating an annual communications plan, then I suggest you give it a try, because the process itself enables you to clarify your vision, discover a new set of possibilities, have a blueprint for actions and evaluate your success.

When I earned the Accreditation in Public Relations (APR) certificate[44] from the Public Relations Society of America, the afternoon portion of the all-day examination was to choose one of three scenarios and then write a comprehensive communications plan. We studied for months prior to the exam, memorizing facts and reviewing case studies. We also learned a really nifty step-by-step process that broke sections of a plan into achievable, bite-sized pieces.

44 http://www.praccreditation.org/apply/apr/

The acronym that gets me through the creation of a communications plan is R.O.P.E., which stands for research, objectives, planning and execution/evaluation. It's a reminder of the order of operations, specifically that research and knowing what your objectives are must always come first before you dive in and start thrashing about, which, unfortunately, is what most people do.

If your fiscal year starts on January 1, then it's not too early to start your planning in June. There are some media outlets, particularly magazines, that plan their shows and issues many months in advance, and so it should be with you. We don't always have the luxury of time, but ideally, we ought to be thinking about the coming year as much in advance as possible.

The Need for Research

In actuality, we're always doing research—watching the market, getting customer feedback, observing behavior, monitoring our online media channels, etc. We need to understand the hearts and minds of our stakeholders as best we can so that we can establish mutually beneficial relationships and achieve our objectives.

Through research, we gather insight. The more data we collect and the more people we talk to, the deeper and more accurate our insight will be.

Doing research helps us remember to think beyond ourselves and that we are not the centers of the universe. Remember the "spotlight effect?" Research reminds us to stop drinking the Kool-Aid[45], because it's toxic. Too many businesses and products fail because of the lack of consideration of what the target market actually wants and needs.

Steve Jobs was famously misunderstood when he claimed not to have done market research. He said, "People don't know what they want until you show it to them. That's why I never rely on market research. Our task is to read things that are not yet on the page." This quote has been

45 https://en.wikipedia.org/wiki/Drinking_the_Kool-Aid

misinterpreted by many to mean that market research is unnecessary[46] when you're developing something new.

Doing research helps us remember to think beyond ourselves and that our business is not the center of the universe—our customers are.

Jobs and his team did quite a bit of market research. His team studied consumer and user behavior in depth. They concluded that people liked computers, but found them confusing. People liked music, but were frustrated by their MP3 players. Based on research and observation, they were able to create something that delighted the marketplace.

When Apple products were on the drawing board, the Jobs team asked people one-on-one their opinions of certain product features, and then tweaked accordingly. Jobs did research that made him an expert on how people engaged with technology. He walked a mile in their moccasins and understood the pain points.

Consider the Ford Edsel story. The "Edsel" has gone down in history as an epic marketing failure. The story appears in textbooks as how *not* to create and launch a product, and why we need to rely upon, and correctly interpret, market research.

In the 1950s, Ford spent significant time and resources conducting polls and collecting surveys, but they ignored the feedback. That was their first mistake, and it led to a devastating cascade of calamity that cost them millions in losses, such as:

They created consumer excitement for the product before launch. It's great strategy to get people excited about the forthcoming release of a product, but in this case, Ford shot itself in the foot. In ignorance of consumer need, Ford invested in an elaborate publicity and advertising "teaser" campaign to create buzz and ignite curiosity. A year before launch, they promoted the E-car (short for "experimental"), promising it

46 https://www.linkedin.com/pulse/steve-jobs-research-quote-should-rip-bob-gilbreath

was an innovative car of the future. None of the ads showed pictures of the car, so consumers were left to picture it in their imaginations. When the curtain rose and the car was revealed, the public was sorely disappointed. It was a big, ugly, malfunctioning mistake on wheels, and critics panned it, even made fun of it.

The Edsel was designed by a Kool-Aid-drinking committee. *Time* magazine called it, "irrational groupthink." The Edsel designers focused on designing a vehicle for a segment whose needs had already been met with other Ford products.

The name, Edsel, didn't resonate with audiences. An ad agency submitted hundreds of catchy names, but the company chose instead to name the car "Edsel," in honor of Henry Ford's son, against even Henry Ford's objections.

They misinterpreted the research. The Ford Company spent many thousands of dollars on market research. What they didn't know then was that people tend to lie on surveys, telling researchers what they think others, not themselves, want. Some argue that the survey data was viable, but Ford disregarded the findings and interpreted it incorrectly.

Worse, the Edsel had many mechanical flaws. The assembly lines had trouble putting it together. There were complaints about the tail lights. The worst feedback of all, however, was about the appearance of the front grille. One of the nicer insults was that it looked like "an Oldsmobile sucking a lemon," and there were other snarky anatomical references.

Thus, the Edsel didn't sell. In contrast, the Ford Mustang was a huge marketing success, and Lee Iacocca is credited for having understood the needs of a younger generation who wanted something sporty.

During the research phase of your communications plan, you must step back and take a deep look at who you really are in the eyes of your target audiences. Are you authentically bringing something important to the world, something your target audiences actually want and need? The only way to answer these questions is to go outside and ask them. Consider other things besides just "product." Evaluate how your product or service is delivered, the attractiveness of your personal brand, your competition, the environment, and your S.W.O.T.—strengths, weaknesses, opportunities and threats. Try and find common interests between yourself and your audience, gaps in perception and needs that are going unfulfilled.

Types of Research

As I mentioned in Chapter 9, there are two types of research: secondary and primary. ***Secondary research*** is an evaluation of the mountain of data that's already out there, i.e., books, articles, research, etc. Most people stop here, satisfied with the avalanche of useful information, but despite the abundance it's only a part of the picture. ***Primary research*** is about the data you collect on your own through intercept interviews, experiments, behavioral studies, surveys, questionnaires, exit polls, mystery shoppers and focus groups, to name a few of the options.

There is also ***formal*** research, and ***informal*** research. Formal research conforms to rigid standards and is used mostly in academia. The research results are published or peer-reviewed, and contribute to the pool of human knowledge and understanding. Informal research is the collection of information that helps us better understand the behavior, thoughts, beliefs, feelings and attitudes of our target publics, i.e, market research, so that we can make educated assumptions. All of the research we'll discuss in this chapter is ***informal*** research.

Primary research can be expensive, which is why many businesses rely heavily on the secondary data. Big brands spend hundreds of thousands of dollars to hire research firms to do statistically valid explorations of customer attitudes and behavior. Much of the cost is in the labor required to collect and analyze the data. Some research, including political polling, requires the need of a large sample size in order to be considered valid. The more people you interview, the less the margin of error. For example, a sample size of 1,500 yields a three percent margin of error.[47]

---

47 https://www.isixsigma.com/tools-templates/sampling-data/margin-error-and-confidence-levels-made-simple/

However, there are research options that don't require heavy investment other than your time, such as **surveys** and **opinion** polls you send using a free online survey tool. This kind of data collection is most effective—and more newsworthy—when your sample size is large and the results are particularly interesting.

Be prepared for low response rates on surveys. Some companies offer an incentive to make completing the survey more attractive. For example, if people provide their contact information on the survey, they'll be entered into a drawing for a coveted prize. The highest response rate I ever got—40 percent of a 4,000 sample size for a whopping 1,600 responses—was when we surveyed bank customers age 65 and older via snail mail and enclosed a crisp, $1.00 bill in the envelope. Senior citizens, most of whom are on a fixed income, liked getting the money. My CEO wasn't too thrilled about that.

During the research phase of your communications plan, you must step back and take a deep look at who you really are in the eyes of your target audiences.

Surveys give you an intuitive feel for what the target audience believes, feels or knows, but these results are only the tip of the iceberg. One of the big takeaways from the Ford research debacle is that people aren't always honest in surveys, or they're giving you information that they think you want to hear. In other words, the results can be unreliable. The best research for small- and mid-sized businesses ought to be conducted face to face.

Focus groups give you the opportunity to interact with specific audiences in an intimate, informal setting. It's when you bring eight to 12 people into a room to solicit their feedback or initiate discussions. To get the most reliable, honest information from the participants of a focus group, you should consider adhering to a few best practices:

* Hire a professional focus group moderator. It takes skill and training to manage a group of chatty (or reticent) people and keep them

on track. There are times when certain individuals monopolize the conversation (there's always one), and times when some individuals won't speak at all. A good moderator knows how to ask the right questions, elicit participation, manage the motor mouths and encourage full participation.

* Hold the session in a neutral location, such as a local conference room or a facility created specifically for focus group sessions. The latter is wired for sound and video, and has a two-way mirror so that the client can watch the session unobserved.
* They mustn't know that they're participating in a focus group to talk about you or your business in particular. You can't invite friends or family and hope to get honest opinions. Authors who have shown their book manuscripts to their mothers and best friends have learned this the hard way. *It's so goooood,* they'll say. Despite their loving intentions, it doesn't help you. It's best to invite strangers to a focus group, anonymously. To prevent bias, participants mustn't know that they're talking about a specific business, only that they're giving opinions in the most general sense. For example, if you're a local upscale restaurant owner who's building a stronger brand, a question might be, "What do you consider to be the nicest five restaurants in the area? Why?"
* Keep the group size manageable. Up to 12 is ideal. Any more than that, and the discussion grows increasingly difficult to manage. You want everyone to have the chance to speak frankly.
* Offer an incentive to entice people to participate. Feed them, pay them or give them something you know they'll really like. I've done several focus groups for clients who wanted the opinions of doctors or CEOs, and we had to make it very worth their while in order to get them to participate—nice buffet dinner, lovely facility, a round of golf at a posh local club. It's most customary to pay focus group participants outright, anywhere from $50 and up. Some groups will do it for pizza. It all depends upon your target audience.

The main point is, don't jump blindly into the creation of a product or service without first knowing that there's a market for it. Once you've established that you're filling a need, ongoing research helps you to keep tabs on your performance, i.e., whether you're satisfying those needs, if you're well thought of, if you're keeping up with your competition, if employee morale is good, and if there are any unmet needs you can satisfy. Avoid the "white tower" syndrome, which is when the CEO, (the one who is barricaded from the real world by layers of management, board directives or self-serving shareholder interests), or business owner (who spends too much time working "in" the business rather than "on" the business) has no idea what's going on in the minds of employees and customers.

Objectives

An objective is a specific business goal you would like to achieve over the next 12-month period. The objectives listed in your communications plan should support the objectives listed in your business plan. For example, if your business goal is to increase revenues by 20 percent by December 31, 20xx, your communications plan will set out ways to help accomplish that rise in revenue with communications strategies.

Business objectives aren't necessarily concerned with increases in revenue. For example, if a construction company wants to install a large, noisy rock crusher on a site, they must apply for a permit, which will only be granted if certain conditions are met. If there's the risk of a significant community uproar, the permit may not be granted. One of the objectives of the communications plan, therefore, will be to establish positive relationships with influencers (legislators, bordering homeowners associations and city council) to increase chances that the permit will be granted.

Focus groups give you the opportunity to interact with specific audiences in an intimate, informal setting.

An objective is specific and measureable. Are you familiar with the S.M.A.R.T. acronym? It's a mnemonic device to help you remember how to set your objectives: specific, measureable, achievable, relevant, time-bound. *I will sell 10,000 copies of my book by December 31, 20xx.*

I don't want to make this too complicated. Most of us are small businesses (97.9 percent[48]) and our objectives are usually straightforward: We want to make money, build a product or service, sell that product or service, open a new location, get more media attention, achieve a five-star rating, etc. We also might want to improve employee morale, launch a new annual fundraising event or change our name. These are all major initiatives with many moving parts and they must be planned out to the last detail.

Pick three critical objectives you would like to achieve in the coming year, and pour your heart and soul into them. Don't take on more than you can manage with your existing time and resources, or you'll spread yourself too thin.

Your objectives should be ***specific.*** *Sell my book* is specific. They should be ***measureable***: *10,000 books sold.* Is the goal of selling 10,000 books ***achievable***? It's a stretch, but it can be done with intense effort. Your communications plan will explain how you'll accomplish it. Is this objective ***relevant*** to the growth and success of your business? Is it worthy of priority attention? In this example, it certainly is if you're an author, speaker or subject matter expert. ***Time-bound?*** Having a specific deadline makes a difference in the level of effort you'll apply to the achievement of your goal. In project management, we establish a date of completion and then plan accordingly by working backwards.

Target Audience and Messages

There are three different types of audiences you'll need to identify as you think through your publicity and content marketing plans over the next

48 http://sbecouncil.org/about-us/facts-and-data/

12 months: primary, secondary and tertiary. All of these audiences are important, and you need to know where they fit so that you can strategize accordingly.

Your ***primary*** audiences are those from whom you want the most important action, for example, to buy your product, sign up as clients or attend your event. A ***secondary*** audience helps us get through to the primary audience. The media is a secondary audience. Kids are often a secondary audience. We plan campaigns targeted to children, but our real intent is to get to the parents, who may be your primary audience. The third audience to consider is the ***tertiary*** audience. These are, for example, the chambers of commerce, Rotary clubs and other professional associations that give you access to primary or secondary audiences.

As I may have mentioned before, there's no such thing as "the public" where business strategy is concerned. There are many publics, which we break down by calling them "target audiences." Here's a partial list: customers, prospects (hot leads, warm leads), employees, the neighboring homeowners association, shareholders, vendors, suppliers, journalists, parents, boomers, bikers, botanists. It's important to be very specific. During the research phase, you will have made important discoveries about who your primary, secondary and tertiary audiences are. There will be nuances, classification systems, and further segmentation and refinement down the line as you're implementing your plan. You may even discover a new species, which, in turn, will beg for revision of messaging, or you'll be inspired to create new products or services, new humans to serve. Choose the three audiences who fit within your bandwidth. The first choice is easy: journalists. The other two are those who are most likely to help you achieve your stated objectives.

It's not enough to say that you target "women" or "men." Skilled communicators and marketers are able to pinpoint a target audience exactly. The notion of the "audience of one," or "avatar" are buzzwords of digital age marketers. Your primary audience, therefore, might be a recently divorced single mother between the ages of 40 and 55 whose kids are about to leave the nest. Or, your avatar could be someone age 65 and older living on a fixed income, just scraping by, who drives weekly from bank to bank searching for the highest CD interest rate and has accounts all over town.

Once you've settled upon your most important target audiences, it's time to determine what you want to say to them, what actions you'd like them to take, or what behaviors you'd like them to change. And, you'll select a set of core, ***key messages*** to which you believe each avatar will respond, because it'll seem like you're talking directly to them—which you are.

When we were trained to write a communications plan for the APR certification exam, we learned to approach things in threes, e.g., three objectives, three target audiences, three key messages for each audience, etc. You'll have fewer or more depending on what resources you have available to communicate frequently, consistently and effectively with each. Just one audience can keep a solopreneur busy for a lifetime, but you'll never have just one audience. The minimum number of audiences you can have is two, because one of them is the media. This is a default setting that cannot be deleted (like the automatically installed Apple Watch app on your iPhone 5.)

Can you *not* include the media as one of your target audiences? Sure, but it will be to your detriment. It's the driving reason behind the writing of this book. I'm here to save you from perennial obscurity. I bring you fire.

Your primary audiences are those from whom you want the most important action, for example, to buy your product, sign up as clients or attend your events.

Accordingly, create three key messages for each target audience, the beliefs about your brand that you want them to have, what you especially want them to know about you, what behaviors you want them to adopt, who you are, what you do, how you impact the community, etc.

Your key messages keep everyone on track and focused on the mission. They guide the creation and curation of relevant content. They keep you focused during media interviews. They tell you what to say in those fateful moments when you're asked to explain what you do for a living.

Remember to flow back to your mission critical objectives so that you can better pinpoint which audiences are most likely to help you achieve them. I say this because in my 30-year career as a professional communicator who helps businesses achieve their goals, I've seen a lot of time- and money-wasting activity amongst the small business population, or, the improper allocation of scarce resources. If there's something you're doing that's not going to affect or build relationships with your target audiences or not directly tied to your mission and objectives, drop it.

Strategies

Once you've done your research, established objectives and identified your target audiences, it's time to create a plan of action. According to the rule of three mentioned above, you will have up to three strategies for communicating with each target audience.

Don't confuse "strategy" with "tactic." A tactic is one piece of the strategic puzzle, because every strategy has a ton of moving parts. A tactic is one wheel under the wagon, one finger on the glove. The strategy explains how you will achieve a given objective.

Let's say you're a subject matter expert with an objective to sell 10,000 copies of your self-published business book by December 31, 20xx. Even though it's January 1 and you seem to have plenty of time, it's still a tall order. That's okay! Big, hairy goals get the adrenaline flowing.

You'll need to get the word out to a lot of people to hit that target, and you have about six dollars in your pocket after you've paid off your editor, cover designer, printer and distributor. How will you do it? Some of the most obvious strategies, all of which live under the public relations umbrella, are:

* Launch an aggressive, three-tiered publicity strategy:
    1. Build your brand as an expert by fostering mutually beneficial relationships with the members of the media who are

interested in your topic. Be a selfless contributor of story ideas and opinions.
2. Secure interviews on talk shows (radio, TV, podcast) and relevant print media
3. Get reviewed by book reviewers in traditional and digital media outlets

* Secure and promote speaking gigs
* Create, curate and distribute great content
* Build a strong online platform, i.e., a loyal, devoted fan base

All of the above strategies will win you, the author of a ground-breaking business book, the potential to get in front of many thousands, perhaps millions of people, which ties back to your objective of selling 10,000 books within the next 12 months.

Tactics and Timeline

There are hundreds of tactics available to you in the wonderful world of public relations. To keep us focused, let me remind you that public relations concerns itself with "earned" media (press coverage, TV appearances, etc.) and "owned" media (your website, blog, YouTube channel, etc.), which means you don't pay for the exposure you get. "Paid" media falls under the marketing umbrella, and includes pay-per-click, display ads, Facebook ads, commercials, billboards, etc. If you wish to include "paid" media in your marketing mix and you have the resources, go for it! It greatly increases the chance of hitting your sales target.

Staying true to our example objective of selling 10,000 books, the list of tactics might look like this for the first strategy listed above:

Strategy: Launch an aggressive, three-tiered publicity strategy

1. Build your brand as an expert by fostering mutually beneficial relationships with the members of the media who are interested in your topic. Be a selfless contributor of story ideas and opinions.

Tactics:

A. Develop a list of pertinent media contacts
B. Become familiar with their work to understand their beat, style, deadlines and previous work
C. Reach out via phone, email and if possible, in-person
D. Monitor breaking news and industry trends and offer insight when possible. (a.k.a. "newsjacking.")

2. Secure interviews on talk shows (radio, TV, podcast) and relevant print media.

Tactics:

A. Create an online press kit (include list of interview questions)
B. Develop a list of television and radio talk shows and podcasts; research names of relevant contacts at each
C. Listen to all shows to become familiar with content and style before making contact
D. Get media training
E. Reach out via email and phone to pitch interview
F. Get reviewed by book reviewers in both traditional and digital media outlets[49]
G. Research book reviewers and follow their submission guidelines
H. Have both PDFs and books on hand, ready to send
I. Write and send query letter
J. Follow up politely
K. Thank them for their review

Evaluation

In this part of your communications plan, you'll explain how you'll determine your strategies and tactics have been yielding the hoped for results. Do a reality check quarterly. Take your plan's pulse. In the first two

49 http://www.writersdigest.com/editor-blogs/there-are-no-rules/marketing-self-promotion/how-to-get-reviews-for-self-published-books

quarters, measure success against the types of things you needed to do to get your plan off the ground in the first place.

You'll need to create a ***timeline*** for your 12-month plan, which is a schedule of when certain tasks must be accomplished. In the first couple of quarters, check that all your tasks were completed in the allotted time. This in itself is a measureable result.

After six months, take the pulse of your communications to your target audiences. Are you getting any traction at all? Have you made good relationships with media contacts? Are people commenting on your blogs or engaging with your social media posts? I would be asking myself, am I on track to book 24 speaking engagements this year? If not, what do I need to do differently? How can I adjust my sails to catch the right wind?

The Barcelona Declaration of Measurement Principles

A group of esteemed PR professionals got together in Barcelona, Spain in 1995[50] to talk about a pressing topic in the industry, which was how to measure the results of public relations to demonstrate its viability and effectiveness in the corporate setting. This think tank developed the following list of seven critical qualifications.

1) You can't measure it if you haven't set a goal.
2) You ought to be measuring the results you've achieved, not the amount of work it took to get you there.
3) What effect did the PR program have on business results? (Did favorable press coverage inspire your target audience to buy your book?)
4) Count your press clippings, and observe what was said about you in each. If you got 100 mentions, but they all said bad things about you, that's not good. If, however, the mentions were mostly good, then that's a result you can be proud of. In the olden days, PR firms would tell their clients that they got 100 press mentions, but

50 http://www.instituteforpr.org/barcelona-declaration-of-measurement-principles/

then stop there. That's why the Barcelona Declaration says that media measurement requires quality in addition to quantity.

5) This qualification is about AVEs, which is an abbreviation for "Advertising Value Equivalent." We used to tell clients, "Hey, you got a 10 column inch article in the *New York Times*. A display ad of equivalent size would have cost you $5,000 dollars. Therefore, you achieved an AVE of $5,000 dollars." The Barcelona Declaration does not condone this as a metric for measuring PR effectiveness.
6) Social media is now viable as a measure of PR success. That's a good thing, because social media is fairly easy to measure.
7) This one gives us a success measurement that is just as viable in the world of science as it is in public relations, and that is, the campaign you used can be used again and again with comparable results.

Will you ever need to measure your PR program with this caliber of metrics or sophistication? Perhaps, if you're working within the frame of a large organization that insists you produce metrics in order to demonstrate a tangible effect on the bottom line, but otherwise, you will generally know when a strategy is or isn't working. All I ask is that you give it time to work. Don't bail after six months. Sometimes it takes months, even years to build to the tipping point. Keep grinding.

Take the Chapter 17 Quiz

Score 100 percent on every chapter quiz for your chance to win free tuition for the PR Breakthrough™ Publicity Boot Camp:

http://bit.ly/2fFyHtY

Chapter 18

Do You Have What it Takes?

"Nothing in this world can take the place of persistence. Talent will not; nothing is more common than unsuccessful men with talent. Genius will not; unrewarded genius is almost a proverb. Education will not; the world is full of educated derelicts. Persistence and determination alone are omnipotent."

— *Calvin Coolidge*

"If you're not making someone else's life better, then you're wasting your time. Your life will become better by making other lives better."

—*Will Smith*

If you're reading this book, it may mean that you're frustrated because, despite your best efforts, your message isn't being heard, or acted upon, as extensively or at the level you'd like—or at all. Your flickering candle flame is continuously being blown out by the breath of millions of others who want the same things you do, whatever those things may be. The rise of the Internet has made it worse. Yet, you know there's a way for that flame to become a roaring fire if you could only find the right accelerant.

Perhaps you're reading this book because you're an individual who has an "idea worth spreading."[51] You're on a mission to enlighten and serve others, but you realize you're just a tiny speck floating helplessly in a thunderous whirlwind of noisy wannabes. You have faith, though, that somehow you can make your voice heard above the roar of the crowd, and the right people will eventually hear you and collect into an audience of millions. After all, countless others, some of whom aren't half as smart or talented as you are, have crossed the boundary that separates the struggling unknowns from the widely recognized.

Perhaps you're reading this book because you have a business that's not attracting or engaging enough people. You've spent lots of time and money on marketing—advertising, social media labor costs, newsletters, networking—but you can't seem to move that needle. You haven't implemented a publicity strategy, either because you don't have the knowledge or skills, or you don't see the value. And yet, you're curious. You see your competitors are doing those things with great success, perhaps stealing away business that should have been yours, and you've decided to step up to the plate, or at the very least, see what's involved. You're hoping it'll turn out to be less difficult than you thought.

Have faith, that you will make your voice heard above the roar of the crowd, and that the right people will hear you and collect into an audience of millions.

Success is within your grasp when you realize you live in a world where everyone's interconnected by virtue of our most basic similarity: our humanness, and our intrinsic need to communicate. To say that one has communicated effectively is to say that one has caught the attention of, and had a positive impact on, another human being, or—better yet—with

51 http://www.ted.com/about/our-organization

millions of human beings. To get widespread exposure through publicity—which serves to activate and attract human energies and magnetize them to your message—you *must* find a way to plug into that interconnectedness. *That* is the heart of public relations. You succeed when your brand resonates with, and delivers value to, the audiences that need you—the ones you're meant to serve.

This ***notion of interconnectedness*** isn't as woo-woo as it may sound. Your ability to understand the needs of your target audiences, to step away from the Kool-Aid long enough to walk a mile in their moccasins, and work to build mutually beneficial relationships, depends on it. It requires a level of self-awareness and knowledge of the psychology that drives human behavior. Actually, it requires several things.

If you hope to win the trust of your audiences, fill your pipeline with leads and build a solid reputation, you need to be able to answer "yes" to the following questions:

Do you have the talent? This is a brutal question, but remember, there is a broken heart for every light on Broadway.[52] Anyone who's ever watched open auditions for a talent contest knows that there are people who walk onto the stage who are, as American Idol's sometimes-cruel Simon Cowell famously exclaims, awful! Everyone has dreams. Many are called to do certain things, but few are chosen. Are you very, very good at what you do? Does your company have something truly special and unique to offer? Have you built a dream team of talented people who can pick up the slack on the areas where your skills are inadequate? *Journalists like to interview and tell stories about talented people.*

Do you have the passion? Passion is what keeps you in the game when sometimes it seems all hope is lost. People with passion are excited about the road they've chosen and the slow climb rarely feels like work. Passion allows you to stretch yourself—to push through fear and take bold action. People can feel your passion when you describe your vision or what you do for a living. Passion is attractive. If you don't feel passion in your business,

52 https://youtu.be/7NgTnomj_bg

you must find a way to ignite it by bringing more of yourself into it. Without passion, your talent is useless. *Journalists like to interview talented, passionate people.*

Are you persistent? Building relationships and earning widespread word of mouth takes time and consistent effort. There is no such thing, for example, as a "one and done" publicity campaign. There must be many publicity campaigns, many relationships to build, many content placements, on and on, breaking through one barrier, and then another, slowly but surely gaining momentum and feeling ever closer to your goal. There is no "there," though. Public relations is a way of life, a daily practice that's integrated into the fabric of your business and the core of your consciousness. It is the oxygen of your business's capacity to expand. To stop breathing is to cease to exist. *Journalists like to interview talented, passionate people who never give up.*

Do you keep learning? Ten years ago, Web 2.0 didn't exist. Rapid technological innovation is a fact of life. Ten years from now, even five years from now, the business landscape will have changed dramatically. Augmented reality applications like Pokemon Go have achieved unprecedented popular success and thousands more apps like it are poised to hit the market. Virtual reality is in its infancy, but it's coming. Futurists predict that much of the content and journalism of the future will be produced by artificial intelligence, and that, in fact, some of that is happening now.[53] Our challenge is to keep ourselves up to date on anything that's going on in the world that affects the hearts and minds of our target audiences. We must keep ourselves commercially viable, too. Spend a little time each day expanding your knowledge and personal development. *Journalists like to talk to talented, passionate and persistent people who have helpful insights and opinions to deliver.*

Do you have a service mentality? Are you dedicated to providing value in order to build loyalty and trust? Showing that you care about people's well-being goes a long way in establishing a strong brand and reputation. It's best practice to give tirelessly of your expertise in service to others. Journalists appreciate when you send the occasional note to

53 http://relevance.com/will-artificial-intelligence-kill-content-marketing/

let them know something's going on in which they might be interested, regardless of whether it serves you personally. Customers and prospects value the content you provide that helps them increase their knowledge or improve their skill set. It's karma. Some pundits say that 75 percent of your communications should be for the purpose of providing value. *Journalists like to have relationships with talented, passionate and persistent people who behave the way trusted colleagues do, which is to help each other out. No one likes to feel used, including the media.*

You succeed when your brand resonates with, and delivers value to, the audiences who need you—the ones you're meant to serve.

Are you creative? Can you be fresh and original? Can you create publicity campaigns and story ideas that are interesting and relevant to your audience? Publicity is an art, and publicists are artists, and sometimes magicians who are able to conjure something out of nothing. Publicity requires a fertile imagination, technical skill and the ability to inspire great numbers of people to take action or change behavior. It is alchemy—transforming lead into gold. The publicist is a craftsman who pulls together seemingly unrelated items to create works of beauty and significance. *Journalists like talented, passionate and persistent people who know how to breathe new life into the mundane.*

Keep lighting your candle. Your flame burns hot, and it gives light to those who seek to find it. Now go—your public awaits.

Take the Chapter 18 Quiz

Score 100 percent on every chapter quiz for your chance to win free tuition for the PR Breakthrough™ Publicity Boot Camp:

http://bit.ly/2foJdr8

About the Author

Dana Dobson is an award-winning public relations consultant, journalist, author, speaker and trainer who helps leaders, businesses and brands tell their stories to the media.

Dana is the creator of the PR Breakthrough Publicity workshop series, a comprehensive and entertaining online training program that shows you how, step-by-step, to create your own successful publicity campaigns. She is also the host of the Media Pro Spotlight podcast, featuring interviews with top media professionals who willingly share tips and advice for working with the media effectively.

Dana speaks frequently on building market presence for executives and subject matter experts, demystifying media relations and how to write effectively. To have Dana come and speak to your group, send an email to: dana@danadobson.com.

Glossary

AP Stylebook — A writing style guide for journalists. It is published and updated annually to reflect changes in writing style and news guidelines. It provides fundamental rules for spelling, language, punctuation, usage and journalistic style.[54]

Advertorial — An ad in a newspaper or magazine that looks like a flattering editorial piece but is actually an article that has been paid for.

Breaking News — An event that is happening and being reported on *now* by media outlets.

Burying the Lead — Failure to provide the most important information at the beginning of a news story or press release.

Chinese Wall — The impenetrable barrier that separates a media outlet's advertising department from the editorial department. It is meant to preserve editorial integrity and unbiased reporting. It prevents conflict of interest that arises when advertisers attempt to secure editorial coverage by virtue of the money they've spent on advertising.

Content Curation — Publishing or passing along articles and content that may be of interest to the target audience. Used as a social media strategy to increase the volume of online activity and as link-backs to other sources.

Content Marketing — The placement of your original articles and content in other channels or outlets such as magazines, newspapers and a plethora of online sites to build brand and improve SEO.

Crisis — A reputation-damaging event, or emergency situation within your sphere of influence, or for which you are responsible, when human

54 https://www.apstylebook.com/

lives, the environment or damage to property are at stake. Examples are industrial accidents, workplace violence, natural disasters, criminal conduct, public protests, etc.

Daybook — A television newsroom's schedule of which stories will be covered each day.

Earned Media — Attention given to you by media outlets without your having paid for it. Usually refers to publicity.

Editorial Calendar (Magazine) — A calendar magazines prepare that shows the focus of editorial content in each issue throughout the year.

Foundational Content — Passages of text that can be cross-purposed and reused in several other items of content, e.g., white papers, bios, company backgrounders, etc.

Key Messages — Statements that relay the most important points you want your audience to understand and retain. Ideally, there are three: The first explains the issue, the second describes the problem, and the third explains the solution.

Lead — The first and most important paragraph of a press release. It provides the who, what, when, where and why of your story. Usually 45 words or fewer.

Media Kit — Not to be confused with "press kit," this is a compilation of information that magazines put together to provide information to advertisers. Sometimes the editorial calendar lives within the media kit.

Media Relations — The function within public relations that establishes and maintains mutually beneficial relationships with journalists and information gatekeepers. Media relations creates a two-way exchange of communication. The goal of media relations is to secure positive coverage or mentions in the myriad of relevant communications channels.

Newsjacking — Newsjacking is the process by which you inject your ideas or angles into breaking news, in real-time, in order to generate media coverage for yourself or your business.

News Pyramid — A.k.a. inverted pyramid, a diagram used to illustrate how information ought to be organized in a news story, with the most critical information on top and narrowing to the least critical information at the bottom.

Newsworthy — Worthy of being reported as news, in a journalist's opinion.

No Comment — Don't ever say this to news media. It's a cue that you're hiding something.

Not for Attribution — A term used during an interview with a journalist indicating that you do not wish your name to be associated with a given quote. May appear in a news story as, "... a source close to the White House said..."

Nut Graph — The paragraph in a press release that explains why a story is newsworthy.

Off the Record — A term used during an interview with a journalist which is meant to be kept in confidence and not used in the story.

On Background — Information given to a journalist during an interview that is useful for the story but not meant to be attributed to you in any way.

Owned Media — Media properties, or modes of communication, that are within your control and operation, i.e., website, blogs, email, podcasts, videos, etc.

Package — A package is a self-contained taped news report. Many networks use news packages to provide innovative newscasts to broad audiences.[55]

Paid Media — Promotional exposure (space, air time, editorial) that you pay for; it's advertising.

Pay-for-Play Editorial — Advertising that's disguised as objective media coverage. Many local/regional lifestyle magazines, for example, sell space in their publications; the articles are "advertorials." It's not "media coverage."

Press Kit — A collection of material that helps journalists and vested stakeholders gather information about you and your business quickly and easily.

Press Release — Written as a news story in AP style, this is a vehicle for making a newsworthy announcement. It is sent over the wire or directly to a media outlet with hope your story will be passed along by that outlet.

Primary Audience — Your ultimate end user. These are the people with whom you wish to engage directly, and from whom you want the most important action, for example, to buy your product, sign up as clients, attend your event, donate money or receive your information and act accordingly.

Publicity — A public relations strategy that seeks to attract the attention of your target publics by securing wide and significant mention in the media, word of mouth or other types of communication.

Public Relations — Public relations is about creating, curating, managing, distributing and marketing content to support and promote

---

55 https://www.thebalance.com/what-exactly-is-a-news-package-for-a-tv-newscast-2315185

initiatives, attract target audience attention and develop brand loyalists. [56] It establishes and maintains mutually beneficial relationships upon which your success or failure depends. (Cutlip, Center & Broom)

Secondary Audience — The people who influence the primary audience, such as the media. Every plan should target secondary audiences. Kids influence parents, or vice versa. Wives influence husbands. Neighbors and friends may be secondary audiences.

SEO — Search engine optimization. It's a Web 2.0 term that describes the use of keywords on your website or content in order to achieve high rankings by search engines or attract more visitors to your site.

Social Media — Internet slang describing channels of electronic communication through which users create online communities to share information, ideas, personal messages and other written, visual or auditory content.

Target Audience — The group of people, or public, from whom you wish to extract desireable actions or behavior.

Tertiary Audience — The audience that gives you access to your primary or secondary audiences, such as chambers of commerce, clubs or professional associations.

Traditional Media — All forms of communication that existed before the internet: newspaper, magazine, television, radio, newsletters, etc.

56 Marie Alonzo, http://smallbiztrends.com/2014/08/tweeting-public-relations.html

Samples and Resources

Maslow's Hierarchy of Needs

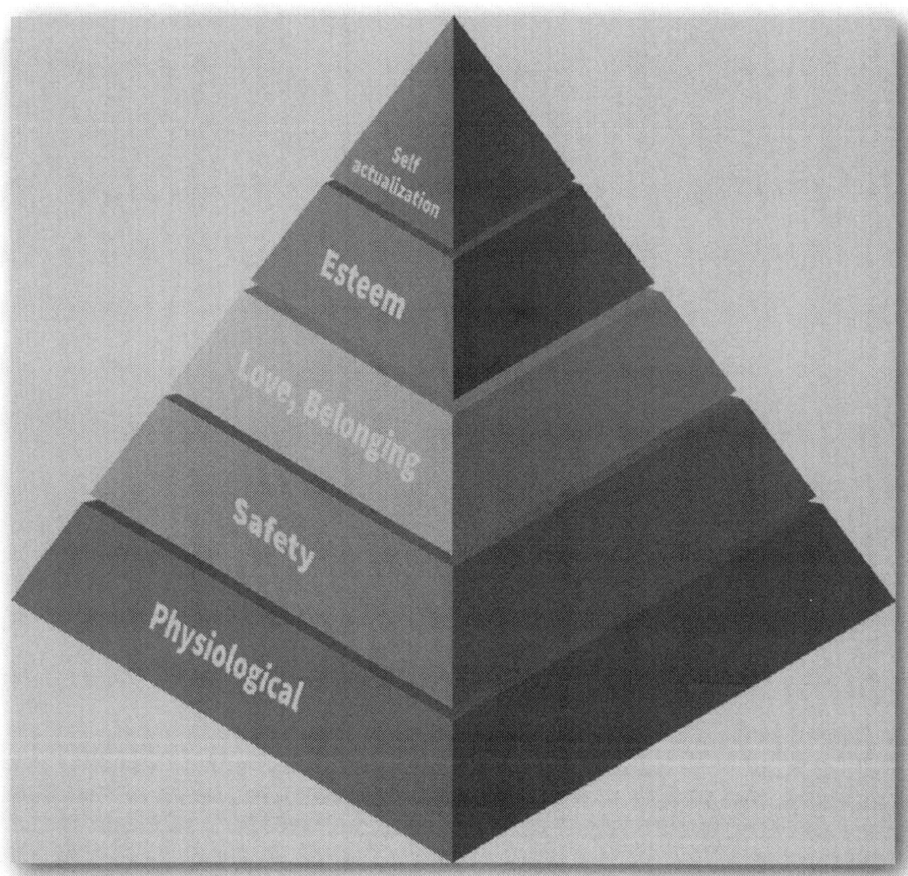

At the base of the pyramid are the physiological needs, which are most essential to keeping our bodies alive: food, water, shelter, and warmth. Once those needs are met, we move up to the next level, which is safety and security: financial, health and well being, and protection from physical harm. Then comes belongingness and love, then esteem, and finally, self-actualization

Press Release Template

FOR IMMEDIATE RELEASE

CONTACT: Dana Dobson
(302) 456-1200
dana@danadobson.com

YOUR ATTENTION GRABBING HEADLINE GOES HERE
Include a subhead that delivers another punch or important info

PHILADELPHIA (Today's date, 20XX) – In this first "lead" paragraph, provide the who, what, when, where, why and how. It summarizes the most important aspects of the event or story. Try to keep it 45 words or fewer.

The second paragraph supplements the above information, providing more of the "why" and explaining why people should care about it.

The third paragraph is a good place for a quote from an important person (the CEO, the spokesperson, the author, etc.), which again explains why people should care about this news story.

The fourth paragraph provides yet more information. If the release pertains to a special event, this is where you'll tell people how to buy tickets and other particulars.

For more information, contact (media contact) at phone number or email address.

About (organization name)

This is the "boilerplate" paragraph. It will appear at the end of every press release you distribute. It is a factual, three- to four-sentence description of your organization and provides readers how to get more information, usually by providing a URL.

###

(These three hashtags indicate the press release is complete.)

Sample Press Release

FOR IMMEDIATE RELEASE

CONTACT: Dana Dobson
(302) 456-1200
dana@danadobson.com

ST. JOSEPH'S HOSPITAL TO HOLD AMBITIOUS FUNDRAISING RAFFLE

First of its kind in the United States; $5-7 million goal

PHOENIX, AZ (February 4, 20xx) — St. Joseph's Hospital and Medical Center will launch a new fundraising project on February 18, 20xx, the first of its kind in the United States. The *Health & Wealth Raffle* has potential to raise $5-7 million for medical education, multiple sclerosis research and patient care at St. Joseph's Hospital and Barrow Neurological Institute in Phoenix.

The raffle offers 7,700 prizes worth more than $4.8 million, including furnished homes, cars, vacations, electronic and recreation prizes and a 1-in-20 chance to win, at $100 per ticket. The idea for the raffle comes from Canada, where similar efforts have been raising millions of dollars for non-profits over the last 15 years.

"Shrinking hospital margins are making it increasingly difficult to fund the services for which we are known," said Linda Hunt, president of St. Joseph's. "I am optimistic that this raffle will provide an exciting new way to raise substantial funds for our hospital this year and in the years to come."

A statewide campaign promoting the raffle will begin on February 18, 20xx. Brochures about the raffle will be mailed to all households in the state. The brochures outline the prizes to be awarded, rules and regulations, and the process for entering. An early-bird drawing for two major prizes will be held on March 31, 20xx, and the final drawing for the remaining prizes will be held on April 28, 20xx.

About St. Joseph's Hospital

Founded in 1895 by the Sisters of Mercy, St. Joseph's was the first hospital in the Phoenix area. The hospital is part of CHW Arizona, a division of Catholic Healthcare West. With 42 hospitals in Arizona, California and Nevada, CHW is one of the largest non-profit health systems in the U.S. For more information, or to purchase tickets call 866-390-9034 or visit www.healthwealthraffle.org.

Sample Frequently Asked Questions

Frequently Asked Questions: *Health & Wealth Raffle*

Q: ***When does the raffle begin?***
A: The *Health & Wealth Raffle* will begin on February 18, 20xx.

Q: ***When is the final drawing?***
A: An early-bird drawing for people who have purchased a raffle ticket by midnight, March 24, 2015, will be held on March 31, 2015. Two raffle prizes, a luxury car package and a dream vacation, will be drawn. The final drawing for the remaining 7,698 prizes will occur on April 28, 20xx.

Q: ***Why are you having this raffle?***
A: With hospitals facing financial challenges, the *Health & Wealth Raffle* may be an important new source of funding for research, medical education and patient care at St. Joseph's and Barrow. Although a raffle like this has never been done in Arizona, The hospital expects to raise $5-7 million.

Q: ***Has this kind of raffle ever been held in the United States?***
A: No. The *Health & Wealth Raffle* is modeled after raffles in Canada that have raised millions of dollars for non-profit organizations for 15 years. It is the first of its kind in the United States.

Q: ***Is this kind of raffle legal in Arizona?***
A: Yes. The hospital has spent many months investigating the concept, i.e. looking into the track records of Canadian raffles, learning about the Arizona laws governing raffles, and statutes related to raffles in Arizona:

> ARS § 13-3302 Nothing in paragraph 1 or 3 of this subsection prohibits a licensed general hospital or a licensed special hospital that is exempt from taxation off income under section 43-1201, paragraph 4 or management, sales or operation of the raffle if the proceeds of the raffle are used to fund medical research, graduate medical education or indigent care, provided that the raffles are conducted no more than three times per calendar year.

Q: ***How will the proceeds of the raffle be used?***
A: Proceeds from the raffle will support medical education, research and patient care at St. Joseph's Hospital and Medical Center and Barrow Neurological Institute. A large portion will be used to establish a research program for multiple sclerosis at Barrow.

Q: ***Who has ownership of the list of purchasers' names and would they be used for any other purpose by the raffle manager?***
A. All names of raffle purchasers after the close of the raffle belong exclusively and confidentially to St. Joseph's Hospital. Prior to the close of the raffle, the list may be used again to do a second mailing.

Q: ***Who is eligible to purchase raffle tickets?***
A: In order to participate in the *Health & Wealth Raffle*, the entrant must be at least 18 years of age. The raffle is intended for residents of Arizona and for out-of-state residents only if they are physically in Arizona at the time of ticket purchase. Board members and executive management staff of St. Joseph's Hospital and Medical Center and Barrow Neurological Institute, employees of Bearing Point and their family members living in the same household are not eligible to purchase tickets.

Q: ***How many tickets will be sold?***

A: Only 150,000 tickets are available for sale. 81,000 in ticket sales is needed to break even.

Q: ***What are the odds of winning a prize?***

A: The chances of winning are 1-in-20. This number has been verified by the Department of Mathematics and Statistics at Arizona State University.

Q: ***How do I purchase a raffle ticket?***

A: Raffle tickets will be for sale beginning February 18, 2015. Brochures, which will be mailed to every household in the state, will outline the prizes to be awarded, rules and regulations, and the process for entering.

Sample Fact Sheet

Fact Sheet: *Health & Wealth Raffle*

A Winning Combination in Support of Healthcare in Arizona

* The *Health & Wealth Raffle* begins February 18, 2015, with the final drawing on April 28, 2015.

* A total of 7,700 prizes—worth more than $4.8 million—will be raffled. No prize is valued at less than $100 retail.

* Proceeds from the raffle will support medical education, research and patient care at St. Joseph's Hospital and Medical Center and Barrow Neurological Institute. A large portion will be used to establish a research program in multiple sclerosis.

* Only 150,000 tickets are available. The chances of winning are 1-in-20, which has been verified by the Department of Mathematics and Statistics at Arizona State University.

* Raffle participants have the chance to win more than one prize. The winning tickets will be drawn by computer. After each ticket is drawn, the name of the winner will be recorded and the number returned to the draw.

* An early-bird drawing for two prizes will be held on March 31, 2015. Tickets purchased by midnight, March 24, 2015 will be included in the drawing. These tickets will also be included in the main drawing on April 28, 2015.

* The main drawing for the remaining 7,698 prizes will occur on April 28, 2015. The cut-off date to enter is midnight, April 21,

2015. Draws will be made from the prize with the lowest retail value to the prize with the highest retail value. In the event all tickets are sold by March 24, 2015, all 7.700 prizes will be drawn on March 31, 2015.

* In order to participate in the *Health & Wealth Raffle*, you must be at least 18 years of age. The raffle is intended for residents of Arizona and for out-of-state residents only if they are physically in Arizona at the time they place their entry. Board members and executive management staff of St. Joseph's Hospital and Medical Center/ Barrow Neurological Institute, employees of Bearing Point, and their family members living in the same household are ineligible to purchase tickets.

* Raffle booklets will be mailed to every household in Arizona (2.5 million households) beginning February 18. A second mailing may occur in March, depending on ticket sales.

* The *Health & Wealth Raffle* is modeled after raffles in Canada that have raised millions of dollars for non-profit organizations for 15 years. It is the first of its kind in the United States.

* With hospitals facing financial challenges, the *Health & Wealth Raffle* may be an important new source of funding for research, medical education and patient care at St. Joseph's and Barrow. Although a raffle like this has never been done in Arizona, the hospital hopes to raise at least $1 million and could raise up to $5 million.

* Winners are responsible for all taxes, fees, assessments and like charges associated with the prize. Sales tax for all vehicles will be covered by the hospital. (For more information, see raffle rules and regulations.)

* The price of entering the *Health & Wealth Raffle* does not qualify as a deductible charitable contribution. The Internal Revenue Service has taken the position that amounts paid for chances to participate in raffles, lotteries or similar drawings for valuable prizes are not gifts.

See official *Health & Wealth Raffle* rules and regulations for more details.

Sample Corporate Backgrounder

In 1895, the Sisters of Mercy opened St. Joseph's Hospital and Medical Center (the Valley's first hospital) with the help of concerned citizens. Since then, the community's ongoing support has made it possible for St. Joseph's to grow to meet Arizona's healthcare needs.

Today, St. Joseph's plays an important role in Arizona's health by providing the highest level of care for serious and complex medical problems. People throughout Arizona depend on St. Joseph's for care of high-risk health issues and life-threatening trauma, and its internationally recognized Barrow Neurological Institute for brain and spine disorders and injuries.

Every year, St. Joseph's invests millions of dollars teaching the next generation of physicians, conducting promising research and implementing cutting-edge patient services. The cost of this research, education and clinical innovation is high. That is why St. Joseph's foundations are constantly looking for new, innovative fundraising ideas, and why it has planned its first statewide *Health & Wealth Raffle*.

The idea for the raffle comes from Canada, where large, multi-prize raffles have been raising millions for non-profits for about 15 years. Frank Leonesio, a member of the Barrow Neurological Foundation (BNF) Board of Trustees introduced the idea two years ago. Since then, the hospital has spent many months investigating the "raffle" concept, i.e., looking into the track records of Canadian raffles, learning about the Arizona laws governing raffles, and assessing the risks and benefits of such a fundraiser to the hospital. After concluding that the raffle's benefits outweighed its risks, members of the BNF Board of Trustees gave their approval to a raffle in February, 2015 to benefit the hospital.

The *Health & Wealth Raffle* is a multi-prize raffle open to Arizonans 18 years and older for $100 per ticket. Prizes will include three luxury homes, 20 vehicles, 47 vacations and more than 7,600 electronic and recreation items—7,700 prizes in all, worth $4.8 million. The chances to win are 1-in-20 or better, depending upon how many of the available 150,000 tickets are purchased.

Net proceeds from this raffle will be used to support healthcare programs at St. Joseph's and Barrow, and to establish a clinical and basic-science research program for multiple sclerosis. For additional information about St. Joseph's Hospital and Barrow Neurological Institute, go to [website address].

Sample Biographies of Key Personnel

BIOGRAPHIES OF KEY PERSONNEL

MEG MALEY, RN, BSN
Co-Founder

Twenty-six of Meg's 28-year health care career have been devoted to improving the lives of people living with cancer. She has founded, owned, operated and sold oncology health care companies and spent almost four years in the technology space as an executive with WellDoc Inc.

Born of her belief that people living with cancer deserve specialized care at home, Meg's first company, Oncology Care Home Health Specialists, was the first and only oncology specific home care company in the country. It delivered hands-on multidisciplinary care for almost 17 years. Now, Oncology Care focuses on delivering a comprehensive, turnkey solution for community-based health care providers seeking to implement cancer specialty programs.

Viewed as a national expert in the field of oncology home care services, Meg has influenced legislation and clinical practice in this sector. She has served in leadership positions on numerous national and local boards and industry specific initiatives over the last 26 years, and has been a founding board member of several thriving non-profit organizations including Cancer Care Connection, a remarkable cancer coaching and referral service.

Since 2003, appointed by two governors of Delaware, Meg has chaired the Environmental Committee for the Delaware Cancer Consortium. She also founded and chairs the Delaware-based "Living with Cancer Fund," which gives financial assistance to cancer patients who are struggling to meet their basic daily needs.

The theme of Meg's professional life has been to ease people's pain and suffering. She derives a great personal satisfaction from helping people through intensely difficult chapters in their lives and guiding them to find meaning and growth from the experiences.

JON BRILLIANT
Co-Founder

Jon is the CFO of Bigfoot Biomedical, whose mission is to provide all people with Type 1 Diabetes (T1D) and their loved ones a reliable, trustworthy, cost effective way to outsource most of the work, worry, and burden of managing the disease.

Prior to joining Bigfoot, Jon was a senior advisor to the Merck Global Health Innovation Fund, where he was responsible for portfolio strategy, opportunity identification, due diligence, deal execution and portfolio oversight.

Previously, Jon was the CFO at WellDoc, where he was also a founding board member. WellDoc makes the only FDA-cleared, clinically validated mobile application that can be prescribed and reimbursed for adult Type 2 Diabetes.

Jon has been a venture capitalist with his own fund (Atelier), a large European fund (Syntek Capital), and a London-based individual investor. Jon has evaluated hundreds of business plans from start-ups to $100 million plus companies, has invested more than $100 million, raised billions of dollars in the public and private markets, and helped restructure the debt of a sovereign country.

In between ventures, Jon has held positions in the health care, automotive and retail sectors. He has also served on the boards of directors of more than 15 companies, ranging from startups to those with more than $500 million in revenue.

With degrees from Duke University and Pennsylvania State University, Jon is a founding member and chairman of the board of Start It Up Delaware, which aims to be the catalyst for creating a vibrant startup community in the state. Jon also serves on the board of directors of Health for America and Opargo.

JILL TEIXEIRA, RN, MSN
Co-Founder

Jill brings more than 24 years of health care experience to CanSurround. She also brings 17 years of executive experience in oncology home health care management and consulting.

As an executive at Oncology Care Home Health Specialists Inc., the first and only oncology specific home care company in the country, Jill was responsible for the development, maintenance and deployment of Oncology Care's clinical body of work (IP) on a technical platform. Additionally, she was responsible for leading a team of national clinical experts in keeping Oncology Care's IP cutting edge. Jill has particular expertise in content management, oncology home care product development, strategic planning and specialty program implementation in the home care, non-profit, outpatient rehabilitation settings.

Jill's work in early phase oncology mobile health (mHealth) application planning provided her a solid background in health care technology. She realized the influence that technology can have in changing patient outcomes for the better and is now committed to bringing technology solutions to those affected by cancer-related distress.

Jill has been a member of the Oncology Nursing Society and has presented multiple times at the local and national levels. She received her master's degree in nursing administration from the University of Delaware in 1998.

Media List Resources

Cision
http://www.cision.com/us/
Used mostly by PR agencies and large organizations (who can afford the pricey annual subscription), Cision maintains a media database of more than 1.6 million contacts, outlets and pitchable opportunities to find journalists, bloggers and social influencers.

EasyMediaList
http://www.easymedialist.com/
Media lists for USA newspapers, magazines, radio and TV stations.

HARO (Help a Reporter Out)
https://www.helpareporter.com/
Help a Reporter Out (HARO) connects journalists with relevant expert sources to meet journalists' demanding deadlines and enable brands to tell their stories. When you subscribe (for free), you'll receive daily emails alerting you of opportunities to contribute your expertise to journalist's queries.

Headline Spot
http://headlinespot.com/
This is a guide to thousands of U.S. and international news resources on the Web.

Internet Public Library
http://www.ipl.org/div/news/
Ipl2 was a public service organization whose website included free access to a database of newspapers and magazines in the United States and abroad. The site is now closed, but the database is still accessible. It is no longer

being updated, however, so be sure to verify the information by visiting the media outlet's website.

LinkedIn
https://www.linkedin.com/
There are thousands of journalists on LinkedIn you can find by using the advanced search feature and using keywords like "reporter," "producer," "talk show," "book reviewer," "business," etc.

List of Blogs that Accept Guest Posts
https://www.effectivebusinessideas.com/blogs-that-accept-guest-posts/
This page contains links to lists of blogs in over 25 categories that accept guest posts. Each category has around 20 blogs listed, making it a total of over 500 blogs; the biggest list of personally-added-and-moderated blogs that accept guest posts online

Media Contacts Pro
http://www.mediacontactspro.com/
This service provides access to comprehensive and current media lists.

List of Podcasts
http://www.stitcher.com/stitcher-list/all-podcasts-top-shows
The Stitcher List is a site that provides lists of the top podcasts by category.

TradePub.com
http://www.tradepub.com/
As the top destination for the latest research and publications, TradePub.com publishes curated resources on behalf of the world's largest and most influential companies. The TradePub.com research library is the #1 resource for professionals to access free research, white papers, reports, case studies, magazines, and eBooks.

Twitter

www.twitter.com

Twitter has a list-building feature. Create a list (call it "media list" if you like). Identify the journalists you wish to follow. Click on the little gear next to the "follow" box and then add them to your media list.

Sample Key Messages

The Future Ready Project
http://www.achieve.org/files/SampleKeyThreeMessages.pdf

* A high school diploma is no longer enough; now, nearly every good job requires some post-secondary education and/or training – such as an associates or bachelors degree, certificate, license, or completion of an apprenticeship or significant on-the-job training.
* Currently, far too many students drop out or graduate from high school without the knowledge and skills required for success, closing doors and limiting their post-high school options.
* All students deserve a world-class education that prepares them for college, careers and life. The best way to prepare students for life after high school is to ensure they graduate with a strong foundation in the core academic areas that will leave all doors open in the future.

Texas Commission on the Arts
http://www.arts.texas.gov/wp-content/uploads/2012/05/Sample-Key-Message.pdf

1. **Art is everywhere.**
   * Art encourages thought and reason, imagination and creativity. Art inspires. Art communicates. Art opens eyes, opens hearts and opens doors.
   * Art and culture permeate our lives through individual and collective expression and experiences.
   * Imagine what your life or your community would be like without art.
2. **TCA directly impacts local economies and culture**.

* State funding for the arts educates children, attracts tourists stimulates business and generates local and regional partnerships - all of which benefit the entire community.
* TCA funding stimulates economic growth by generating tourism revenue, creating jobs and through expenditures of arts organizations toward the creation, promotion and showcasing of their craft.
* The arts are the primary way in which communities preserve and celebrate their culture and heritage.

3. **TCA helps local arts organizations succeed.**
   * TCA supports the arts community of Texas by providing matching funds, tools and technologies, and a committed staff of experienced arts professionals to improve local arts organizations.
   * With reduced state funding, TCA must leverage private dollars to support the arts throughout Texas.

Sample PSA Scripts

National Library Week: Radio Public Service Announcements
http://www.ala.org/conferencesevents/2013-sample-psa-scripts

:15
It's National Library Week! Visit the [name of library]. Communities matter @ your library.
A message from the American Library Association's Campaign for America's Libraries and [name of your library]

:20
Did you know that our library builds its collections and programs to meet the diverse needs of our community? There's something for everyone at [name of library]. Celebrate National Library Week, April 14 - 20. Communities matter @ your library!
A message from the American Library Association's Campaign for America's Libraries and [name of your library]

:30
Today's libraries are driven by the needs of the community. Whether you're looking for e-books, information on student loans or 24/7 homework help for your kids – the [name of library] has the resources to meet your needs and those of the whole community. Communities matter @ your library. Celebrate National Library Week, April 14-20.
A message from the American Library Association's Campaign for America's Libraries and [name of your library]

:30
Community-building connections are happening all the time at your library. From new moms connecting at storytime to small business owners convening to make opportunities happen, to teens meeting up after

school, the library helps foster all types of communities. April 14-20 is National Library Week. Visit your library. Communities matter @ your library.

A message from the American Library Association's Campaign for America's Libraries and [name of your library]

Facebook Group

Artful PR Facebook Community
http://www.facebook.com/groups/ArtfulPRCommunity

This is a FREE discussion forum for people who want to create amazing PR opportunities for their business or brand. Stop by to introduce yourself, and visit often to ask questions, share ideas and provide feedback. I'm in there often, lending a hand. See you there!

The PR Breakthrough™ Publicity Boot Camp

Learn my secrets for …

Mastering the Art of Publicity & Personal Branding to boost your business growth, promotion & success!

Let's face it. While every business strives for success, few achieve it. That's because running a business is vastly different from promoting it. And it's ***promotion*** that's the crucial key to your business success!

Promotion is the art of boosting sales, awareness and credibility for your products and services. And one of the most influential and cost-effective promotional tools is ***publicity.***

By using publicity strategies you can build your brand, reach ideal prospects and dramatically grow your business.

I know, because I've been consulting with entrepreneurs, small business owners and executives on these success strategies for more than 30 years.

Now I've put together all the wisdom, insights and "tricks of the trade" into one exceptional program – my **PR Breakthrough™ 6-Week Publicity Boot Camp**.

It's the fastest … smartest … most effective way to have all you need to know about publicity at your fingertips – including answers to your pivotal questions – from a PR pro with a proven track record of success.

Through this Boot Camp I'll show you how to:

- Get valuable publicity perks for your business
- Generate the press coverage you deserve

- Communicate so editors respond to your emails
- Save thousands of dollars wasted on ineffective advertising

In fact, you can forget advertising, trade shows -- even direct marketing. The best bang for your business marketing buck is publicity ... but *only* if you know what you're doing.

Unfortunately, most companies don't know the secrets of effective publicity!

They make foolish – and often costly mistakes – sabotaging their efforts to attract new customers, boost brand loyalty, and build lasting relationships with existing customers. Many are innocent mistakes based on poor timing, simple oversights or infractions of media protocol that can be easily remedied – once you know the "rules!"

With my tell-it-like-it-is **PR Breakthrough Publicity Boot Camp**, you will discover how to put your company or yourself on the map -- and rise above the competition.

My **PR Breakthrough Publicity Boot Camp** is the online version of a live classroom series. The entire curriculum has been tested and vetted by an impressive roster of business professionals: marketing directors, CEOs, authors, solopreneurs, start-ups, new business owners and seasoned veterans.

I can say with absolute certainty ... if you do the work, you will succeed. You will see results, have amazing experiences – and make promotion fun!

The 6-module group coaching program starts with an Introductory Orientation module. Then I'll send you a new module every week. Each module includes an intro video, slide presentation, a video presentation by a member of the media, homework, handouts, and a closing video with a spark of humor. The homework is designed to give you practical, hands-on experience with the materials. In some assignments you will be preparing actual documents you'll need for your business publicity program.

In addition, I review all of your assignments and give you personal feedback. You can email me at any time with questions or comments.

My comprehensive Boot Camp Program includes ...

Your Weekly Group Q&A Call

Each week we will have a live one-hour Q&A call to dive more deeply into the week's subject matter. You can submit questions in advance. The call is always recorded for your added convenience.

Your One-on-One Private Coaching Call

You also receive a personal one-on-one private telephone call so you and I can chat about your business and get to know one another better. This is my favorite part of the entire boot camp!

Your PR Breakthrough Client Forum (Facebook)

Our Client Forum is a private closed group exclusively for PR Breakthrough members. You can brainstorm and share contacts with like-minded professionals who understand the tools and power of media relations. Ask questions. Share opinions. I'm there regularly and always happy to help.

Your BONUS: Answer my movie trivia questions

In the introductory video for every module, there's a quote from one of my favorite movies. Answer my questions about which movie the quote is from, which character said it, and what actor played that role and I will give you an extra 60 days of PR coaching! That includes a free 45-minute private telephone consultation, and review of new media relations documents you create.

Think of me as your business PR partner – the one to bounce ideas off, who won't judge your master plan, who will guide you on the journey to becoming proficient with publicity and media relations (maybe testing the reality of some of your assumptions along the way)!

"The value I received from Dana Dobson's PR Breakthrough™ Publicity Boot Camp was exceptional. Her delivery is both entertaining and effective, and the content is amazing. There's a lot of give and take with Dana and my fellow boot camp participants, and it was really worth my time. I can't wait to start applying what I've learned."

—*Elaine Buonopane, M. Davis & Sons, Inc.*

Powerful Proven Success Strategies, Tips & How Tos in 6 Weekly Modules …

MODULE 1: Newsworthiness – Stories That Grab the Media's Attention

When you fully understand what kinds of stories journalists consider "newsworthy," you'll no longer be baffled as to why editors ignore your press releases. You'll discover the 12 news determinants, why they matter and creative ways you can create a fountain of great story ideas for you and your business.

MODULE 2: Creating the Irresistible Press Kit

The press kit is an essential tool you'll use again and again for publicity campaigns and media relations. You'll discover the dos and don'ts of what works for every press kit, and start customizing your kit during the workshop.

MODULE 3: Demystifying the Media
Crucial steps in why and how to develop your own customized media list. Discover secrets to building relationships with targeted media who are interested in your industry and subject matter expertise.

MODULE 4: The Power of White Papers & Case Studies for Your Marketing & PR Arsenal
White papers and case studies are two of the most powerful marketing tools for attracting qualified leads and showcasing your products and services. Get started on creating your own white paper as well as how to repurpose content to attract the attention of your target audiences.

MODULE 5: Personal Branding & Media Savvy
Perception is reality. I'll guide you in creating and mastering your own personal brand to take into the media spotlight. You'll discover how to refine your image and be prepared when the media wants to interview you.

MODULE 6: Preparing Your Communications Plan
This hands-on module focuses on creating a well-researched communications plan, the foundation for all your marketing communications strategies. Discover the best approach to research, objectives, target audiences, key messages, strategies, tactics, timeline, budget and more!

Your 6-Week PR Breakthrough Publicity Boot Camp Package includes all this ...

- ✓ **Access to all six video learning modules** (a $900 value!)
- ✓ **Bonus informational materials** (a $200 value!)
- ✓ **Private Facebook Group**
- ✓ **6 Media Pro Spotlight video interviews (watch members of the media explain their likes, dislikes and how to pitch stories to them)** (a $600 value)

- ✓ **Supervised and reviewed homework assignments to create publicity materials** (a $600 value)
- ✓ **Participation in, and recordings of, live Q&A Boot Camp calls** (a $300 value)
- ✓ **Your Personal Accountability Coach** (a $1,000 value)
- ✓ **60-minute private phone consultation with Dana Dobson** (a $300 value)
- ✓ **Opportunity to earn an additional 60 days of one-on-one PR consultation and coaching**

Plus ... join now & get 2 valuable Bonus Gifts – FREE!

If you register at least 3 days in advance of our next starting date, I will reward you with *two significant bonuses* valued at more than $100!

- ➢ My **MEDIA PRO SPOTLIGHT** EBook: 157 pages of interviews filled with advice, tips, how-tos and mistake warnings from 15 top media experts. A PR "bible" you'll refer to again and again. A $79 value – my gift to you!

- ➢ My **PUBLICITY TOOLS CHECKLIST**: A reference guide that will assure you're covering all your bases every time you reach out for publicity and brand exposure. A $29 value – yours with my compliments!

"Dana's PR Breakthrough™ Publicity Boot Camp was extremely informative. I had very little knowledge of what a press kit was or how to put a pubic relations program together, and now I feel like I really do have the tools and resources to do so."

—*Keyanna Mozie, Delaware Financial Literacy Institute*

NO RISK! YOUR SATISFACTION GUARANTEED!

I've made your participation in our program completely risk-free.
If you're not totally satisfied with the
PR Breakthrough Publicity Boot Camp
after receiving the first module and listening to our first call,
I'll refund your payment – no questions asked!

Reserve your place in the next
PR Breakthrough Publicity Boot Camp –
and get your *free bonuses* – all for just $1,297!

ENROLL NOW!

https://danadobsonpr.leadpages.co/bootcamp-details/

Gone are the days when you can wait for your phone to ring … or hope someone will come along to rescue your business. Your success is in your own hands. But you don't have to go it alone.

With my straight from the trenches insight and advice you'll avoid years of hard-knocks experience to achieve the awareness, authority and media exposure you desire – and certainly deserve.

The **PR Breakthrough Publicity Boot Camp** gives you the tools and knowledge to create and manage a fruitful publicity and media relations program. It helps you develop your "publicity opportunity radar" so you're ready to leap at the right time. With this mindset, diligence and persistence, you will build traction and the momentum to reap tremendous rewards.

Claim your 6-Week PR Breakthrough Boot Camp Package
-- plus 2 bonuses –for just $1,297!

ENROLL NOW!

https://danadobsonpr.leadpages.co/bootcamp-details/

I look forward to meeting and working with you.

Your public awaits!

Dana Dobson

P.S.: If you want the inside scoop on crucial issues such as HOW to get the media to contact you instead of your chasing them … HOW to build on your media exposure so you can exponentially grow your authority and your brand year after year … and much more, join our next Boot Camp NOW! It's a risk-free investment that will deliver valuable business rewards for years and years to come.

ENROLL NOW!

https://danadobsonpr.leadpages.co/bootcamp-details/

"There are people in the world who know their stuff, there are people who really, really know their stuff, and then, there is Dana Dobson, who is an absolute expert! Her PR Breakthrough™ Publicity Boot Camp is exceptional! She gives you so much information and so many great tips for getting your name out there and how to work with the media. I recommend this boot camp highly, and that you choose Dana as your go-to PR expert."

—Angela Jo Manieri, I AM Ministries